along these RIVERS

Poetry & Photography from Pittsburgh

along these RIVERS

Poetry & Photography from Pittsburgh

EDITED BY
JUDITH R. ROBINSON
MICHAEL WURSTER

QUADRANT PUBLISHING, LLC
PITTSBURGH, PA
2008

Along These Rivers

Printed in the USA by Herrmann Printing
Pittsburgh, Pennsylvania

Copyright © 2008 by Quadrant Publishing, LLC

Quadrant Publishing
Pittsburgh, Pennsylvania

Catalogued by the Library of Congress
ISBN 978-0-9800545-0-7
Library of Congress Control Number: 2007942849

Cover Art by Philip Pearlstein
Front: *Greenfield Hazelwood,* 1948, gouache on board
Rear: *View from Hazelwood,* 1948, watercolor

Cover Design: Judith R. Robinson & Jason Michael Bacasa
Design and Book Composition: Jason Michael Bacasa
Photo Editor: David Rohm

The Editors wish to thank Silver Eye Center for Photography,
Pittsburgh 250 and The United Jewish Federation of Pittsburgh.

Contents

Preface
MICHAEL WURSTER

Introduction
JUDITH R. ROBINSON

KATHRYN AYRES
Gothic / 19

MARILYN BATES
Sonogram, May 2, 2000 / 20

JOAN E. BAUER
On a Flight to Cedar Rapids / 21

CLAIRE BAUERLE
Skunk Cabbage / 26

RUTHANNE F. BAUERLE
Photograph / 51

JAN BEATTY
Going Deep for Jesus / 22
Pittsburgh Poem / 25

PETER BLAIR
Friday for the River / 27
Oakland Hospital / 28

ANITA GEVAUDAN BYERLY
Steam Rising / 32
Braddock Avenue / 34

RICK CAMPBELL
The Candles at Margaret Mary Catholic Church / 35
*How the Streets in Front of Kaufmann's Department
    Store Tell Me I Am Home* / 36

JAY CARSON
Baking the Ginger Boy's Tongue / 39

ANNABELLE CLIPPINGER
Autumnal / 40

HAZEL COPE
July 12, 1904 / 41

FERRIS CRANE
Photograph / 115

JOHN R. CUNNINGHAM
Steeltown, 1956 / 42

ANNE CURRAN
One Blue Basket / 43

JAMES DEAHL
The Nature of Light at Bar Harbor / 46

TOI DERRICOTTE
Before Making Love / 52
On Stopping Late in the Afternoon for Steamed Dumplings / 53

ANNETTE DIETZ
Aria / 58

BERT DINMAN
Photographs / 45, 145

PATRICIA DOBLER
Effigy / 54
Juarez, 1978 / 55

BARBARA EDELMAN
Dream of the Gone From City / 59

ZIGGY EDWARDS
Hope's White Shoes / 60

SUE SANIEL ELKIND
Jerusalem of My Dream / 61

TIMONS ESAIAS
Would I Give the World, All of It, for Love? / 62
Lines Written to an Unknown Audience,
        Waiting for the Night's First Act / 64

RINA FERRARELLI
Mushrooms / 65

CHARLES FERRARO
Photographs / 17, 137

GAIL GHAI
Lunch on the Monongahela / 66

JACK GILBERT
A Fact / 68
The Danger of Wisdom / 69

LOIS I. GREENBERG
Cross-Country, 1951 / 72

AARONEL deROY GRUBER
Photographs / 67, 89

GRACE GUNDERMAN
She Wanted a House / 74

BEN HARTLEDGE
Landscape of Frozen Voices / 77
The Beautiful Girl / 78

TIM HEMPFIELD
Godzilla! / 79

RUTH ELLA HENDRICKS
Photographs / 71, 157

DOROTHY HOLLEY
On the Subject of Beauty / 80
Photograph / 81

MIKE JAMES
Poem Dictated at Kazansky's Deli / 82

MARC JAMPOLE
Schoenberg's Second Conversion / 84

REBECCA JUNG
Basil & Scotch / 83

BRIAN KALDORF
Photograph / 56

MIKE KANE
Prayer of Pulling Down Bricks / 86

JOSEPH KARASEK
Bending Scooping Bending / 90

ROMELLA KITCHENS
Morning Meditation / 96

NANCY KRZTON
On Pittsburgh as Poet's Canvas / 98

ANDREA LONDON
Photographs / 63

BRANDON McCHESNEY
Photographs / 30, 31, 38, 57, 131

BERLIN MEMOR
Photograph / 162

MARGARET MENAMIN
Kate Soffel Writes to Her Husband from Jail / 102

CHRISTINE DOREIAN MICHAELS
China Blue / 103

VIVIANA MIHELCIC
Triumph / 104

DAN MOHAN
Photographs / 24, 100, 151

STEPHEN MURABITO
Blessings, Cursings: The Chained Shelves / 106
In Love with the B-Girls / 108

ED OCHESTER
Pasta / 109

WALT PETERSON
Shaking Hands with a Jackhammer / 112

LAURA PETRILLA
Photograph / 76

GRACE RISHELL
Intermezzo / 114

MARK ROBERTS
Photographs / 94, 95

JUDITH R. ROBINSON
In Stilettos / 116

SANFORD N. ROBINSON, JR.
Photograph / 105

ROSALY DEMAIOS ROFFMAN
Translating Color: A Primer / 118

DIANE R. ROSE
Photographs / 121, 147

MICHAEL ROSE
Time Warp / 120

MICHAEL D. ROSELLA
Photograph / 50

SANKAR ROY
Good Folks / 122
In Search of My New Country / 123

JOANNE SAMRANEY
Even at Five / 124

MIKE SCHNEIDER
Breath Through Bones / 126

NATE SCHRITTER
Photographs / 101, 110, 111

DANIEL M. SHAPIRO
The Messenger / 125

GERALD STERN
Rose in Your Teeth / 130

SHIRLEY S. STEVENS
On Gobbler's Knob / 132

RICHARD ST. JOHN
from *Christmas Requiem* / 128

CHRISTINE TELFER
Fool Moon Over the Mon / 133

PHILIP TERMAN
Lost Dog / 134

ESTHER JACOBSON TUCKER
Sleep / 136

BERNADETTE ULSAMER
Pulling a Piano Out of the Pond / 138

PETER M. VERCILLA
Photographs / 70, 127

JUDITH VOLLMER
Field Near Rzeszow / 140

LYNN WAGNER
Glass Case No.1: Want / 144

M.J. WASHINGTON
What I Liked About Home / 146

ARLENE WEINER
The Maladroit / 148

LORI WILSON
I Sat on the Rock with My Sleeves Rolled Up / 149

REBECCA WINTERS
Photographs / 44, 119

JACK WOLFORD
Pell-Mell Dune / 150

MICHAEL WURSTER
John Deere / 152

HUANG XIANG
The Wisp of Light / 153

JUDY YOGMAN
April / 154

MICHAEL W. YOUNG
Twilight Innings / 156

ANDRENA ZAWINSKI
Driving the Laurels / 158
Photographs / 85, 159

VINCENT ZEPP
Endymion / 160

BOB ZILLER
Carson St. Epiphany / 163

CONTRIBUTOR NOTES / 164
ACKNOWLEDGEMENTS / 172

Preface

In 1989, Bennington Press published *Living Inland*, a collection of photography and poetry by Pittsburgh area women, edited by Judith R. Robinson. Three years later, in 1992, The Squirrel Hill Poetry Workshop, spearheaded by Sue Saniel Elkind, came out with *Pittsburgh And Tri-State Area Poets*. That's it. Despite being a vaunted poetry city, Pittsburgh, host to a number of fine literary and poetry publishers and both academic and non-academic poetry programs, has not been represented by a comprehensive poetry anthology since 1992. ¶ Judy Robinson and I had talked for some time of doing a new anthology of Pittsburgh poets. Finally the stars and planets aligned themselves properly around the 250th anniversary of the city of Pittsburgh. Thus, the volume you hold in your hand. As in Judy's 1989 book, we've included photography. ¶ We put out a call for submissions and received a tremendous amount of fine work, so much in fact, that many wonderful pieces did not "make the cut" and had to be left out due to space considerations. There are a number of poets included who were unknown to us. It's also true that, for whatever reason, some of our well known poets did not submit work. If we failed to get the message to them we apologize. We have included several poets who no longer actually live in our area, but who have remained Pittsburgh-identified. We have also included three deceased poets who remain our contemporaries. ¶ Of course, Judy and I believe that our choices reflect some sort of objective aesthetic standard. It's also true that personal taste always enters in. Other editors might have made other choices. At any rate, we hope readers love *Along These Rivers* as much as we loved putting it together.

— MICHAEL WURSTER

Introduction

The inspiration to produce (this collection) springs from the sense that something wonderful is happening in the area of expression at this time, in this place... The reason for assembling the collection reflects an equation, aspects of which concern time, place and people... ¶ So I wrote in the introduction to *Living Inland,* an anthology of poetry and photography by women, published in 1989. ¶ The factors present then are even more abundantly with us today: we are alive in a place of civility, Pittsburgh, Pennsylvania, now in 2008, our city's 250th anniversary year, and this time around, in *Along These Rivers,* our intent is to be more completely representational. ¶ The fact is that the Pittsburgh area is, and has long been, home to a large and lively community of gifted artists, particularly poets and photographers. Many of the artists represented in this anthology have achieved national and international reputations; their work is, by popular as well as critical review, outstanding. Equally exciting are the talented newcomers just emerging in these pages, all young and gifted. Special mention and profound thanks go to painter Philip Pearlstein, 20th Century Master of Realism, and native son of Pittsburgh, for gracing this book with his cover art, "Greenfield Hazelwood" and "View from Hazelwood." We also wish to thank David Rohm, photography editor, and Jason Bacasa, graphic designer. Without their fine contribution this book would not have been possible. ¶ *Along These Rivers* represents the work of 92 artists—poets and photographers—48 women and 44 men. From A for Katherine Ayres to Z for Bob Ziller, clearly neither gender has exclusivity on talent or initiative. What they do have is the shared experience, the exceptional rootedness—of Pittsburgh. ¶ We know that our region has been blessed with 250 exciting years of history—it is a fact that the history of Pittsburgh profoundly parallels and intersects with so much of the history of America—as well as a richly realized, unique cultural heritage. ¶ We are a center of higher learning, as well as a place of ethnic diversity and great energy. Surrounded by rolling hills and filled with interesting neighborhoods, rivers and bridges, we can also lay claim to one of this country's most beautiful skylines. ¶ We share such abundant blessings in this nurturing little city, not the least of which is our community of artists. ¶ So it is with pride and love for Pittsburgh and its environs, and pride and love of the arts of poetry and photography as practiced by the special individuals you will discover in these pages—that Michael Wurster and I present *Along These Rivers*. ¶ Happy 250th Anniversary, Pittsburgh!

— JUDITH R. ROBINSON

CHARLES FERRARO

GOTHIC

as in a cheap gothic
morning fog seeps
across the lighthouse road
feathers edges
obscures trees

a slender man
emerges
atop the rise
a ghostly
presentment

what fiction
to a lone
woman
in a rented car
on an empty road

lover? villain?
then I see the leash
only
a country man
out with his dog

KATHERINE AYRES

SONOGRAM, MAY 2, 2000

"She looks like ET" — Dr. Michaels

Little Alien,

In this private window I have invaded, you take
that first step onto the landscape of my cratered heart.
Your tiny ear cocked on the other side, listens
when the doctor puts his trumpet to your mother's womb.

You hear every flung note of your father's guitar,
your mother's giggles as he explores
the full moon of her stomach, searches
for the signal of your own morse code.

O little satellite strung from the moon, you already know
much more than mere earthlings, holding all the world's seeds
in the tendrils of your fingertips. Maybe birth stops
our knowing, steps us back light years from what we knew.

When Archimedes geared the universe in a tiny box, you were
that little mirror turning on the axis of the earth.
You are the slung stone, a red sari, the flattened A of arias.
You are Gallileo's gasp at the firmament.
You are September and the last placid days of plenty in the womb.

Soon a game little heart will launch you from your watery nursery
into the bounty of a distant ocean — A father to protect you
from the Great Bear, a mother whose own beauty
turns back the sun, waiting to hear the music of the spheres
when your bright voice breaks the room.

MARILYN BATES

ON A FLIGHT TO CEDAR RAPIDS

All the new poems are about loss.
Freud knew: how from the first, our hopes are thwarted.
The squirming body: baby-lips suck-suck,
but the bounteous breast moves on.
How in our dreams, the floorboards fall away
and our loved ones forget they even know us.
We are flying west at 30,000 feet, and I remember
growing up, knobby, obstinate, squelchy
with the dampness of my dreams.
I think of Levertov: *I know this happiness is provisional.*
It is just that Joseph is beside me, reading a mystery,
and wearing the purple corduroy shirt. We are floating
on a thin broth of clouds, above a green patchwork,
with roads like curving threads. And I wonder:
Is that a shallow lake? Is that a flood plain?
I say, *They should give you a shirt that reads—*
"Joseph, the famous poet from Pittsburgh,"
He shrugs me off, *Too many famous poets.*
And I give him a little squeeze, and he says,
No fondling on the airplane. Below the trees
are dark moss, and we are entering the clouds.

JOAN E. BAUER

GOING DEEP FOR JESUS

Run to the street light, make a right
at the blue car, and go deep
— Sharon Watson

1981, I'm on the back of a cherry
red Kawasaki with my boyfriend Stush,
my biker jacket bought with a tax return
from a year of waiting tables, stuffed
in my pocket the bad check I wrote
to see Stevie Ray play the Decade.
Down Beck's Run we hit Carson, my cheek
resting on Stush's firm shoulder till
the ground rises up with the hulk of J&L
across the river, steel house that burns it all,
an up-against-the-wall-fuck, thick &
ripping, everything is smokestacks
& yellow blaze. We ride the river roads,
looking for deserted two-lanes,
newspapers stuffed under our leather
for warmth. I want to forget my name —
everything but the sharp lean into
the next turn, the cheap slap of the wind.
Stush brags about his water-cooled,
two-stroke engine, but I just want
the contact high of leather, metal,
and the slow burn of a few joints.

Past the bridges & bridges, we ride
away from our fast-food jobs and
run-down apartment, toward the smell
of the Ohio, its perpetual mire, the rotting
docks and lean-to's, to what we knew.
I knew the muscles in his back & his
low voice would make me come
back to myself. We stop near the bog
of the river's edge to have hard sex
on the ground, our jeans still on,
trying to shotgun a moment, to split open
our lives in the brilliant light until
we were the mills, we were the fire.
It was then I decided god and orgasm
were the same thing, that if jesus
had an address, it would be a dark two-lane,
if god were here, she'd shove down
like a two-stroke rainstorm,
she'd let it fly.

JAN BEATTY

DAN MOHAN
COREY

PITTSBURGH POEM

On Sarah Street, on the South Side,
the old woman stands with her broom, imagining
the air full of lug and swish from the steelworker's boot,
armies of gray lunchbuckets grace her thoughts
and she sweeps with the part of her that still believes;
sweeps while her sister makes paska and horseradish with red beets,
sweeps away the stains of the dead husband and a disappointing daughter.

She thinks of the dark well of J&L, how it sifted down to nothing,
the mill's hole of a mouth that ate full years of her life,
nights she pulled her husband from Yarksy's bar across the street,
him smiling like a bagful of dimes, half a paycheck spent,
the whole time, soot covering their clothes, the car, the windowsills
like disease, someone else's hands.

She holds tight onto the good times, the new green velour couch,
Saturday walks to the Markethouse for fresh red cabbage and greens,
trips to the Brown & Green store for new T-shirts, South Side windows
brimming taffeta and satin on the way to Mass at St. Michael's,
when the world was gleaming and available for one glorious day.

Now shadows angle across her print housedress and she holds tight
to her broom, hears her sister primping in the kitchen, smells the pea soup
with sauerkraut, the homemade mushroom gravy for perogies, she thinks
of the ten years since her husband died, of her daughter who calls
on holidays, she stands on her concrete lawn,
taking care of something invisible, the listless air,
her life.

JAN BEATTY

SKUNK CABBAGE

Down in a gulch
where snowmelt flows thinly
and quickly over
soil, bypasses
glazed pools
to reach well-
established channels,

they first spring out —
the hoods of half
streaked with iron
red on green,
single – double – triple,
thermal energy
melting rounds —

and you cannot trust
that next time
through watery blues
and browns you
will be able to walk
without a crisp
popping underfoot.

CLAIRE BAUERLE

FRIDAY FOR THE RIVER

After work, you bring a yellow envelope
stuffed with tips from The Wheel Café.
My check from St. Francis Hospital
bears the saint's image, arms raised in prayer.
This week we had two on suicide watch,
and a schizophrenic wrote his name in shit
on the quiet room wall. We stroll into the cold,
windless evening. It's Friday, an illusion
of completeness upon us. Walking twilit streets
to the river, we pass people jostling home
or cramming into happy hours. Light switch on
along the wharf, and the sky's muted blue
corona fades behind Coal Hill.

The river gives back everything
the sky sends down. The bridge arcs
into its reflection, a perfect ellipse of girders.
The hill carries its dark complement,
houses clinging to its underbelly. Along West End,
the lamps set down spikes of light
that shiver in the gloom of the river bend,
the water surface invisible. You lean
against me, your eyes luminous
as the blue water. We look over the levee,
down into a stillness that contains us,
a stillness where a red full moon rises
into the depths of the Allegheny.

PETER BLAIR

OAKLAND HOSPITAL

Her head tilts up against the pillow,
her closed eyes gazing at troubled
dreams as if up into burning rafters.

I sit with her as the sun slips
behind the buildings grappled to Herron Hill,
leaving us in pale window light—

hydrangea sky touched with fingers
of pink. Her hands lift suddenly and flex,
seeming to sign the word pain

through a haze of Demoral. Only pain
could have coaxed her from her house
into the world that took her husband

and son and held her under
self-imposed siege. Even the neighbor's
trees were her enemies.

She gropes at the curls in the sheets,
and smoothes them out like years
as sky-pink fades to snowy violet.

I want to help her hate the disease,
but she can't hear what I can't say.
I sit and read, sneak the Jello

and a hard roll she refused to eat
from her dinner tray. I weeded her backyard
pulling chokers out of dirt,

freeing the hedge, imagining each vine
a cancer lump, hoping each thrump of torn roots
would somehow cure her.

I don't need any other mother now but death,
before which I play like a child
endlessly denying what the parent knows:

that flames consume as they illuminate.
She stirs and groans in sleep. The drugs
wear off, forsake her again in the darkening

paleness of the room. Her eyes open,
gaze at me, then down at her fingers gripping
the sheet-top we've all held

since before we can remember.
I go to her, my hand on her forehead, helpless
as starlight on a burning house.

PETER BLAIR

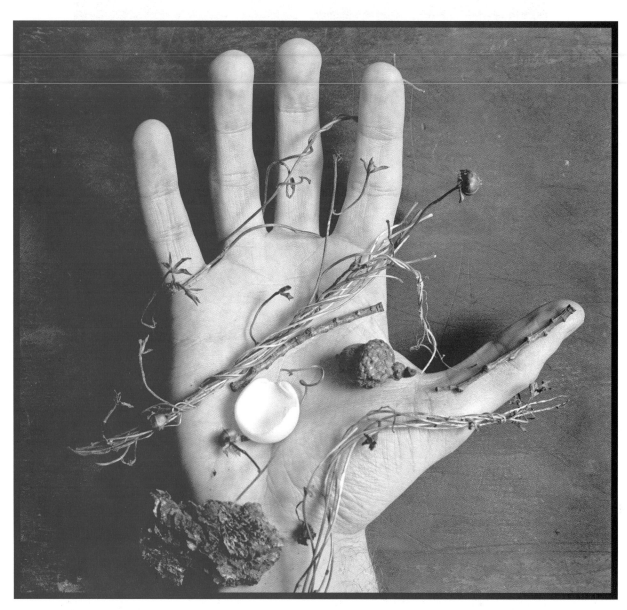

BRANDON MCCHESNEY

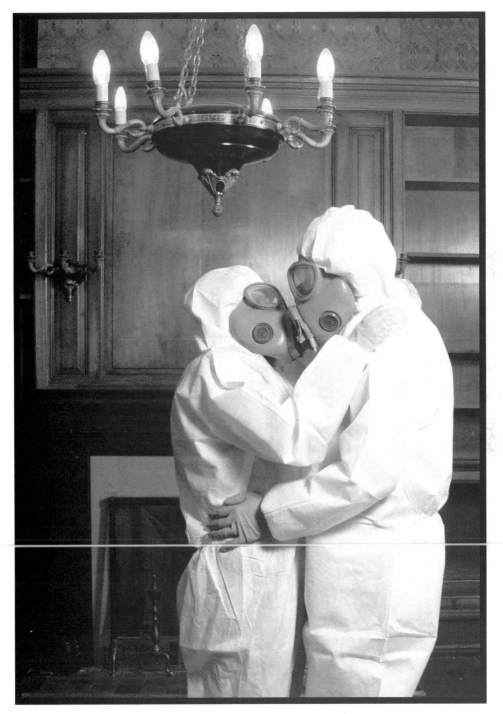

BRANDON MCCHESNEY

STEAM RISING

1

In the winter, downstream, steam rises
on certain street corners like geysers
in Yellowstone, or as if some secret Hades
existed beneath the paved streets.
I know it comes from the heating system
for the high office buildings,
but as I hurry to work, collar
turned up against the wind, I feel
the mystery of steam. Like fog,
it blurs the edges of time.

2

I am saying good night to Jim
on the porch brittle from snow.
He is an ex-prisoner of war;
I am seventeen.
Earlier, his passion had frightened me,
his mouth bruising, his body
asking too much. Now smoke climbs
silently from chimneys; our breaths
rise into the night air,
separate, not mingling.
What do I know about hunger?
What do I know about need?

3

The engine hisses impatiently
as I part from my soldier husband.
Having said everything, we cling together
like an apple being cut apart.
I try to etch his face on my mind, afraid
I won't remember it. He holds me close
under his heavy army coat, and I breathe
in the smell of him, a combination
of shaving lotion, cigarettes, something
intangible. At night I know
I will search for the scent in his pillow.
Steam surrounds me.
I watch, crying, while the train pulls out.

4

As I pour my mother's tea, steam rises
from the old kettle. For years,
we have been the odd couple; divorced daughter,
widowed mother; helpmates, sparring partners.
Now she is slipping a little more each day.
She smoothes the green and white checkered cloth,
stirs the spoon methodically against the cup.
Trembling, she lifts it with both hands, drinks
the hot liquid. Later at bedtime, I take
the steaming washcloth, wring it, hand it to her.
She presses it against her face, against
the parchment skin and closed, clouded eyes.
She tells me how good it feels.

ANITA GEVAUDAN BYERLY

BRADDOCK AVENUE

They'll never come back: two furniture stores,
three banks, three movie houses — Capitol, Times,
and Paramount, where at 13 I let a strange boy
put his hand on my knee, then confessed it
to old Father Joe at St. Mary's on Sixth Street;
and where at 21, a ring was slipped on my finger
while we watched *On the Town* in the dark.

I loved to shop the day before Christmas
at Shub's for fresh roasted peanuts,
the smell catching you before you even got in the door.
I loved to stop at Och's Delicatessen
for corned beef; Nill's for poppy seed bread.
I loved bright lights strung across the street,
green wreaths, decorated trees in the windows—

before Braddock Avenue died, like the mill,
Carnegie's first. Gone are Denardo's Jewelers,
Jaison's, the Famous Department Store,
to the malls leaving boarded doors, blind windows.

Oh, to be there again before black Friday in Dallas
before that long funeral march down Pennsylvania Avenue
with the black riderless horse and the muffled drum cadence
reverberating on *every* Main Street, in *every* home.

Oh, to be back on Braddock Avenue
when our world was was a Saturday matinee,
a dance at the Polish Falcons, where a tall woman
in a polka-dot blouse danced the *schottische*
with a short man in matching shirt, toupee awry.

ANITA GEVAUDAN BYERLY

34

THE CANDLES AT MARGARET MARY CATHOLIC CHURCH

The body parts of 132 souls
are red-flagged with baggage tickets.
I used to sit and stare at the ridge
where the pale sun fell early
and wonder what was beyond it. Later
when I learned about Ohio, Indiana,
the prairies and the mountains west,
I still couldn't believe that my hill,
backdrop to barges working the river,
was the wall between me and the world.

Now, just over the ridge in Hopewell Township
where high, drunk, or both I drove too fast
home from Pudi's or Chuck's, where it was
always too dark when I searched for my turn
down the hill to the lights of the river—
Coraopolis, Sewickley, Aliquippa—
America knows Beaver County now. Wire stories
find these hills domestic: *rolling like the folds
of a blanket of an unmade bed*. They
don't mention the abandoned mills
that were our daily bread, just airplane parts,
flight logs, *deployed thrust reversers*, legs and arms,
tangled in a ravine of hemlock.

Early September, the hills are still green.
From 6000 feet you can see Pittsburgh down river,
the Ohio under your wing, and the land rolling
east dotted with silos and barns.
I could be on this plane flying home,
on a path animated on the nightly news,
and when we fall faster than three rattled Hail Marys,
I would know well what earth rushes to claim me.

RICK CAMPBELL

HOW THE STREETS IN FRONT OF KAUFMANN'S
DEPARTMENT STORE TELL ME I AM HOME

For years I have been lost. Some nights I have known it
        as I looked out at whatever moon hung
over the wrong trees, watched as too-bright stars
        glimmered in a too-clear sky.
Other nights, sometimes for months or years I have thought
        I was home because the land

had grown familiar, because live oak and loblolly,
        palmetto or magnolia had begun to speak to me
in a tongue I understood. I said *I live here*, and the dark angels
        that flitted about my shoulders, tickling my ears
with their doubts, fell silent in front of the beauty of azaleas,
        the mystery of camellias.

But today I see that I have been gone these many years.
        Three days after snow, little rivers of cinder water
run in the gutters, ridges of plowed snow blacken
        where glass and steel cut off the sun. And
in front of Kaufmann's, in the great windows where mannequins
        show us what we *could* look like

my people — men and women wrapped in gray or brown coats,
        carrying plastic bags, lunch boxes, briefcases,
staring straight ahead or into the past — walk the crowded lunchtime sidewalks.
        We dodge each other, snow and ice and running water.
I'm drawn to the deli across the street, to pastrami and Iron City,
        where everyone eating big sandwiches is big

and thick, and their voices sing *Pittsburgh* when they say *Iron.*
   On the street again in the dark canyon
of Grant Street, I head for the river and Mt. Washington rising
   on its far shore. My eyes climb the tracks
on the incline, its red car inching skyward like a bucket of coal
   winched up a cliff. The Monongahela

is running high and fast, spring snow
   runoff carrying trees, beds, chairs,
and trash toward the Ohio, and I know I am home
   because from here on this bridge
I can see the Allegheny's muddy mountain water
   merge with this gray to birth the Ohio. No headwaters,

no springs rising in a quiet swamp of cattails, the Ohio
   rolls full bore past Neville Island's
abandoned steel plants, past the silence of American Bridge,
   past the gravel slab that was once Jones & Laughlin,
past my bedroom window that once saw the fire, smoke
   and ash of three shifts a day, whole valley working,

living mill lives. From here, because I know that I am home
   I can see twenty-five miles downriver as it bends
at Beaver and runs west to East Liverpool,
   where my grandfather bought his shoes and worked his first job,
and then turns south for Martin's Ferry, James Wright, and Wheeling.
   I am home today, all of us

standing in front of Kaufmann's windows, waiting
for the light to change, together at last.

RICK CAMPBELL

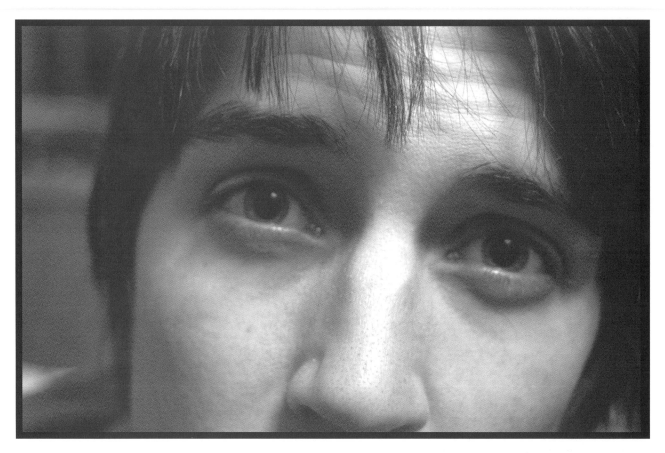

BRANDON MCCHESNEY

BAKING THE GINGER BOY'S TONGUE

"What do you want?"
The white uniformed voice feeds
my anxious sweet hunger, but iced
with the fear of women's words.

"Them, the ones next to," I said.
"Crumb buns? You want crumb buns?
Or the flopovers, which?" Her voice knife sharp
as the red nail of her fingers stabbing at the cakes.

Her ruffled pink collar an old
poisoned plain for her mountain head,
a bumpy nose more sure than Sister Pancratious
smelling out my neck and side sweat.

But my brother warned me
of the rancid taste in feminine scented,
sweet words. And how to lower
to Bogart's lip and tongue swagger.

"I can't give you any until you say."
Her eyes bulge at me,
like muffins rising in the tin.
Finally, timed and done, I rise.

"Crumb buns, crumb buns,"
I cry quickly, through slitted mouth,
cut open for the first of many times,
by the sweet cinnamon of desire.

JAY CARSON

AUTUMNAL

Savor orange, unheeding gentlemen. Let
scarlet pierce you. That angel
knows your name.

May blowing sideways leaves fold you
in where warmth tastes soft,
where water's words rupture the banks
and you can flow along.

Past and past and past, they slide. Taking
with them birthdates and names, gemstones,
in the catapult of value, primed for hurling.

Savor autumn in its bold lettering,
the comfort of bedding in language
entices you past the eye that does not see,
the mound of collapsed vertebra,

past the skull of the bird hidden in leaves.

ANNABELLE CLIPPINGER

JULY 12, 1904

In Chile and in England
on exactly the same day
Pablo Neruda and my mother
entered the world.

He was the poet of love,
and onions,
of passion and lemons.

I think she'd have liked some of his poems if she'd ever read one,
particularly the one about onions.

She liked onions.
"If you put enough onion in a shepherd's pie
you can't tell there's not much meat," she'd say.

I'm not sure she'd have been so keen
on the passion and lemons.

I wonder how the planets were aligned
exactly one hundred years ago today
the twelfth of July, 1904
to have produced two people

different in every way
sex, nationality, genes, and so on
except they both loved onions.

HAZEL COPE

STEELTOWN, 1956

We awoke to the smell
     of steel. An odor,
that we, as adults,
     would label carbides,
  hydrogen sulfide
       & other hazards.
But as children,
     it was the sweet smell
  of our fathers' labors.
It defined our world.
You knew exactly
     where you were
without even
      opening your eyes.

JOHN R. CUNNINGHAM

ONE BLUE BASKET

I can look at the MRI,
the walnut-sized abnormality,
the white inflammation
scattered on grey matter,
nod to the neurosurgeon
and forget it shows
my daughter's brain.

But I look at one blue
laundry basket,
its brittle web
shattered with age.
One blue basket, where
once she curled
sucking her thumb,
needing again the womb
neither of us knew.
One blue basket.
And it grips me as though
this were her broken body,
lying before me.
I couldn't fix it then.
I can't fix it again.

ANN CURRAN

43

REBECCA WINTERS
STAND BY ME

BERT DINMAN
RESTRUCTURED DEBRIS

THE NATURE OF LIGHT AT BAR HARBOR

I

Each day depends so much
on its time of year;
as sunlight shortens,
sea fog clings to inlets
masking lobstermen and boats
as traps are pulled from blackness.

By mid-September clouds hide
the Atlantic; our world's
a pearl-grey watercolour.
Even our tangled sea
lies reduced, its voice
lost in distant pines.

Looking towards town
from the seabucked deck
the light rises from within
like the lustre of pearls.
Every church raises its spire
in hope or certainty.

With hope or certainty
fishermen set out,
voices calling through darkness,
through cold, stone mists.
With luck sunlight might illuminate
Frenchman Bay by noon.

These mornings pass like
lifetimes spent tossing
in heavy swell —
all creation lies mute,
its beginnings lost in shadow,
its end unknowably remote.

How we cling to the present!
Our ship rolls, clouds shift,
the sun catches a steeple
for an instant, then
fades in autumn's stillness
along the battered coast.

II

In the gone days they would sail
for Boston, the Cape
and Nantucket beyond,
small men on small boats
noting that point where
harbour chop meets Atlantic swell.

Never grand, they sought for God within
when sudden squalls
ran inland to toss their
silvered light through clouds
while waves climbed the ripped air
above the grasstopped dunes.

Then the wind would calm;
the men and children would learn
new shapes for landfall
and berry patch. The saltmarsh
would lie down again
between pasture and ocean.

Between pasture and ocean
all is flux. Birds nest in reeds;
rotting foliage scents
the knife-edge breeze,
lingers as the tide runs out,
the flaking rocks cast down.

A hard, stony land
fit for Calvinism's triumph
and collapse;
young men are left to rove the coast,
blown through like autumn fog.
Juniper berries picked

for homemade gin lie fiercely tart
beside the sink. Voices
climb the stairs,
footsteps trace their halls,
hands shut a final door
as design darkens into night.

III

Behind the lighthouse the light
shades from purple to black;
mauve waves run against
a sheer rock face
while up the coast, ragged pines
harvest this dark perfection.

We are drawn to the sea,
to salt and screaming gulls.
Our Earth falls around its sun
causing fire to descend
into water, erotic
and flourishing.

There is no mist this evening
only darkness welling
in the harbour where tied boats
lie in the shadow
of the head. Blue waves bring
goodness and mercy.

Seeking goodness and mercy
the elect settled here
where on magic nights
a blue phosphorescence details
the shapes of waves,
a light rising within.

To them this was Eden
— God's garden on Earth —
and they His chosen ones.
But the honeymoon couples
have long gone home to their
exhausted marriages.

Along the Republic's coast
day fades to night;
Cepheus dies unrescued
in his daughter's place.
We walk these icy coves
to hear the flowers of the sea.

JAMES DEAHL

MICHAEL D. ROSELLA
CLAYTON

RUTHANNE F. BAUERLE
BEACHED

BEFORE MAKING LOVE

I move my hands over your face,
closing my eyes, as if blind;
the cheek bones, broadly spaced,
the wide thick nostrils of the African,
the forehead whose bones push
forward at both sides as if the horns
of new fallen angels lie just under,
the chin that juts forward with pride.
I think of the delicate skull of the Taung child—
earliest of human beings
emerged from darkness—whose geometry
brings word of a small town of dignity
that all the bloody kingdoms rest on.

TOI DERRICOTTE

ON STOPPING LATE IN THE AFTERNOON FOR STEAMED DUMPLINGS

The restaurant is empty
except for the cooks and waiters.
One makes a pillow of linens
and sleeps, putting his feet up in a booth;
another folds paper tablecloths. Why
have I stopped to eat alone on this rainy
day? Why savor the wet meat of the
steamed dumpling? As I pick it up,
the waiter appraises me. Am I
one of those women who must stop
for treats along the way—am I that starved?
The white dough burns—much too hot— yet,
I stick it in my mouth, quickly,
as if to destroy the evidence.
The waiter still watches. Suddenly
I am sorry to be here, sad,
my little pleasure stolen.

TOI DERRICOTTE

EFFIGY

The reluctance of the body
to become a thing...and yet
there are those who wish to be stone.

When I think of his face
I think of effigy, semblance, counterpart,
tracing, copy, I call up a stone mask

over which a fountain trickles, or a
wooden mask, leafy vines coiling from
mouth and eyes. Both could be my father,

quite natural in this landscape, recognized,
familial and alien at once. Had he been given
the choice between tree and stone, I suppose

he would have chosen "tree," even here
in November where the wind probes the gray throats
of steeples, and black barges flatten the river.

PATRICIA DOBLER

JUAREZ, 1978

for R.C.

We were ten years younger, literary,
and when the six bulls, identical, black,
were danced with and formally killed one by one,
it seemed to us the same bull was killed,
the sand raked clean then bloodied by the same bull;
we took this as a sign that life goes on.
Death was a foreign performance, little more
than a reliquary you could hold in one hand,
exotic as a jeweled toe and finger bone
from a sainted Raimundo or Luz.
I'd still believe this if I could, but I have proof
that death is wildly improvisational, informal, someone
who doesn't draw within the lines and he never
does the same thing twice. See here,
the failed machinery of my father's heart.
And there, your slow falling, petal by petal.

PATRICIA DOBLER

BRIAN KALDORF

BRANDON MCCHESNEY

ARIA

Within the only sunbeam
slicing through the forest dark
of thalo green and fallen pine
a single moth is treading light.
I strain to hear its wings
and start to cry remembering
that hollow bones of birds are strong
and weightless of necessity
each gently curving keel
protects a beating heart.
I think of clavicle and scapula
a tiny orbit for each eye
the stillborn notes inside a throat
of downy feathers hitting steel
swift, the silent shredding
that can bring a big plane down.

ANNETTE DIETZ

DREAM OF THE GONE FROM CITY

The problem in the dream is to get home at night
without a car, a wallet or a cent in your pocket.

A route scrolls out like black and white film inside
your head—the boulevard you'll have to walk—

a bulked-up arm thrust miles across the darkened
sprawl: through canyon walls of offices gone black

behind their glass, tunnels under freeways, long
blanks of parks, tenements abandoned to their

boarded up stories, blocks where roots erupt
through sidewalk, where there are no roots, no

sidewalk, paint-stripped houses in raggy skirts
of weeds, street devoid of cars, stoplights gone

meaningless as scattered punctuation. Now
the blurred fast cut, the double image. You're on

the street, walking with your loud heart. Like every
other time, you watch yourself turn into a dark

shortcut. Skinny street, walled in, it's three AM,
and all that intersects is tunnel-like and winding.

Shadows solidify to figures crouched just around
corners. How could you choose it again and again?

Why take the risk? To step into this vicious little detour—no
mace, no money, no image of the home you're walking towards.

BARBARA EDELMAN

HOPE'S WHITE SHOES

Before we moved away,
there was Hope's birthday sleepover;
I sat at a table of laughing ten-year-old ghosts.
Out the window, snow wandered towards asphalt
and the sidewalk heaved up by trees — snow
with the sun still beating
yellow-tinted staccato spun serene
by grazing clouds, bald branches.

Next morning I walked around the corner
to meet the hulking U-Haul as it solemnly ate our couch.
Behind our front-porch snapshot and the four-hour drive
Hope's house stands still
while people stream in and out, blur past
the windows, crowd hallways and steps,
churn into something that's everywhere
and already gone.

When I walk back, I leave time
for that waiting place on Northumberland Street:
the angular furniture, the landscape
painting over the piano, Hope's white shoes
aligned on the doormat.
I sit in dappled underwater shadows
hours after the last of us
sacked out in our sleeping bags.
                    I think I remember hearing them breathe.
Even asleep, they move too fast to see —
their hyperdrive heartbeats, their hummingbird eyelids,
their incalculable dreams.

ZIGGY EDWARDS

JERUSALEM OF MY DREAM

As far as I can see,
there are olive trees,
and green rows of grapes
'til their vines meet the sky;
cucumbers and soft cheese for breakfast.

The hills at sunset turn copper
when the shade comes.
We wake with luminous skins.

I don't know when the dream will end
but, when it does, I hope
the grape arbor is heavy with fruit,
that I will see stones like ruins
crumble in the back yard,
my neighbor's wash drying
in a sun so magnificent
I can find the Red Sea.

SUE SANIEL ELKIND

WOULD I GIVE THE WORLD, ALL OF IT, FOR LOVE?

All the world? Of course, why not?
Who would not give two worlds — Pluto, say,
And Uranus for a glass of melon juice
On any desert summer day?

But should I give the world, this world,
To you? Perhaps you would merely spend it,
Or put it aside, as you did once with my heart
To say only afterwards, the light fading
Into a chill evening, "I forgot."
It is not for me that I tremble,
That I hesitate, but for the world.

TIMONS ESAIAS

ANDREA LONDON

LINES WRITTEN TO AN UNKNOWN AUDIENCE, WAITING FOR THE NIGHT'S FIRST ACT

Outside the sky is lowering the lights
to fit the evening mood.
Inside the early drinks
the ones you can still taste
are in hand, as are the cigarettes.

The problem for me, writing this poem,
is that I don't know
anything about you,
where you are reading this
or hearing this.

By the time I do know, it will
be too late to adjust,
to personalize this poem;
the die cast, and tonight's acts
behind us both.

It is an evening for embracing
the little deaths: the drinks,
the cigarettes, these lines,
the gap between me, at this table,
already in your past, and you.

TIMONS ESAIAS

MUSHROOMS

A strange efflorescence
on the lawn where hidden
roots and stumps
lie below the surface.
Was it the rain, the sun
after rain, the red moon
that caused such profusion?
They glow in the morning
in the silver blue of dusk,
open, and turn inside out
in the bright midday sun—
empty bowls held up to the sky—
split around the edges
into odd-shaped petals.
Smooth and rough
all covered with fragments
of the universal veil.
A few push up close to the ground
without visible stipes
bronze and gold fluted leaves
like coral of the woods
the color of regret.
Edible agarics or poisonous
amanitas? I wish I knew.
There was never a season,
a gathering place.
Our time together short.
Dead in their thirties,
or scattered widely
across two continents,
my people took this
and other kinds of knowledge
with them when they went.

RINA FERRARELLI

LUNCH ON THE MONONGAHELA

The way a redwing blackbird appeared so abruptly on the green
railing fence next to the gilded river, the way the shy sun suddenly

bolded as it rolled a bright gold ring of fire into a sky aching with cyan
and silver, this burst of colors, sashay of shapes, could have been

a Parisian painting: *Luncheon of the Boating Party* brushed with velvet
edges, black netted hats and the woman with gauzy auburn hair,

buttermilk flesh, pouting burgundy lips, leaning in the foreground,
the woman Renoir will marry. In the sky of brie and cobalt, we could

be a couple balanced on that boat sipping along the Seine. You suited
with a black top hat, I draped in pastel flowers. But this is Pittsburgh.

This is the Monongahela, blackish green as the slag heap that spills
its dark history into the summer swift current. This is the Waterfront

at Homestead. It's June, and the afternoon sunlight is brutal, but
welcomed after days and days and days of dampening gray rain.

I let the heat come, rays on flesh. It is a pleasure I enter easily.
My bare arms pink into a rosy spoonbill shade, but you have shifted

into shade and shadow. I pour cream for your coffee, a task that seems
intimate as touch. Even the waiter has paused to watch that revision

of colors, black into mocha. To witness these small miracles: how water
darkens to wine; oil spills into portrait. How rivers amber, rust, ice, then green

with seasons. And suddenly like waves, your fingers coalesce into mine.

GAIL GHAI

AARONEL deROY GRUBER
FOG

A FACT

The woman is not just a pleasure,
nor even a problem. She is a meniscus
that allows the absolute to have a shape,
that lets him skate however briefly
on the mystery, her presence luminous
on the ordinary and the grand. Like the odor
at night in Pittsburgh's empty streets
after summer rain on maples and sycamore.
As well as the car suddenly crossing two blocks
away in a blare of light. The importance
of the rocks around his Greek shepherd hut,
and mules wandering around in the empty fields.
He crosses the island in the giant sunlight,
comes back in the dark thinking of the woman.
The fact of her goes on, loved or not.

JACK GILBERT

THE DANGER OF WISDOM

We learn to live without passion.
To be reasonable. We go hungry
amid the giant granaries
this world is. We store up plenty
for when we are old and mild.
It is our strength that deprives us.
Like Keats listening to the doctor
who said the best thing for
tuberculosis was to eat only one
slice of bread and a fragment
of fish each day. Keats starved
himself to death because he yearned
so desperately to feast on Fanny Brawne.
Emerson and his wife decided to make
love sparingly in order to accumulate
his passion. We are taught to be
moderate. To live intelligently.

JACK GILBERT

PETER M. VERCILLA

RUTH ELLA HENDRICKS

CROSS-COUNTRY 1951

"If you've been somewhere, there's no use pretending you haven't."
— Rosaly DeMaios Roffman

1. Alderson, Oklahoma

we stand where
it was — now

a small measure of grass
overgrows a patch of rail

no Choctaws left
only an old black man

my father is silent
waiting to smell

the one-room shack
his father's wagon

Sooner days
no longer on the map

2. Silver Creek, Colorado

My favorite moment
a Colorado hilltop

over the silvermine—
just a tree, me,

& an old cowhand
who offered an 18-year-old girl
a cigarette and his chair.

3. Banff Springs, Alberta

Every moment of surprise—
Canadian sunset, Lake Louise

at High Tea & God Save The Queen,
riding up on the Columbia Ice Fields,

strolling through mountain woods
with a handsome Canadian boy,

my mother strolling down the path
with a man who wasn't my father.

LOIS I. GREENBERG

SHE WANTED A HOUSE

She wanted a house by an eastern sea,
Where the early sun could light bright windows
Over a beach of pale brown sand,
Where she could count the tides as they brought
Fresh weeds and shells and small bright things,
Then left with the tired and the dull and the dead.

Instead, she lived among small hills
In a house with the small and proper windows
That old people and their houses often have.
She had ripped down all the curtains and the blinds
From every glass that faced the south,
For the only tide that she could see
Was the sun that rose and set
A bit beyond the tiresome hills.

She knew that she would never have the sea
To bring the small bright things
She sorely needed to safely sail
The darker tides that swept her soul,
For she was old and nearly poor,
And windows by the sea need youth,
With certain strengths of heart and love—
All things she never had.
But still she prayed that God would see
The hopeful windows straining toward the south,
Defiant in a proper town
Of drapes and blinds and Cape Cod ruffles
Keeping out the light.

Perhaps, even if that tide would never bring
Long strands of seaweed dripping salt and shells,
She could some day, somehow, ease through
The southern-yearning glass
And sail into her own sweet sea
Where the moon-drenched tide goes on forever,
Filled with small bright gifts from God.

GRACE GUNDERMAN

LAURA PETRILLA

LANDSCAPE OF FROZEN VOICES

Night clouds

                                            unfurl

                  over
                  the soft hill

          vent
          shafts

          blow

               long vowels
               of smoke

               the moon
                    an ember

smoldering
        behind the vapors

BEN HARTLEDGE

THE BEAUTIFUL GIRL

The beautiful girl with the tapered snout.
The beautiful girl with the German engineering
       who suns on an I-beam,
       who begets a burning tire.

The beautiful girl under the factory smoke
       with the neck screw & the fiery eye.
The beautiful girl at 7:15,
       a fire extinguisher in drag.

After coffee break, the beautiful girl
       lights cigarettes, flashes her blue eye.

Through the day, she goes hissing, emptying her lungs,
       licking every seam.

BEN HARTLEDGE

GODZILLA!

King of the Behemoths, gust chunks of a mountain
into dark nightfall sky toward the moon
like some lizard-lycanthrope from beyond sky,
then puffs fire-breath like a volcano fountain
and puffs his cheeks again to spiral a typhoon
that storms about his huge reptilian eye.
He hangs two waterspouts in tunneled clouds;
ships in the harbor crack with splintery noise,
their flame-draped hulls become burial coffins, howls
of doomed sucked down in rolling sea like bathtub toys.
And now the scaly King may vent his wrath!
His forked-tongue lashes and makes a buzz-saw sound,
uprooting trees and home, he smashes a path—
spits flames at temples on the hallowed ground.

TIM HEMPFIELD

ON THE SUBJECT OF BEAUTY

Beauty does not last
I once wrote in a poem.
But is it true?
In a corner of a yard
by the oak-leaf hydrangea
with leaves now green
stands the dogwood tree,
dark branches still visible
for the leaves are not yet out.

Below sit the daffodils,
now done with their blooming
with ivy snuggled among them.
But the dogwood stands out
in its whiteness day or night.
The white bracts, like crosses,
burst forth. I find my camera,
capture this scene, enjoy
its fragile beauty all year.

DOROTHY HOLLEY

POEM DICTATED AT KAZANSKY'S DELI

"when i lost my job
        my wife threw me out

friends took me in for a while
        first one then the other

later, i slept in my old buick
        and dreamed about gypsies

(backseats never sleep good
        even in summer)

i ate one cheap meal a day
        at tom's diner on carson street

i was skinny back then
        and didn't need much

every day i read the want ads
        and when i finished them

i read through berrigan's sonnets
        and wrote notes on every page

brad let me shower at his apartment
        at least three times a week

it was on shower day that my luck changed
        and someone finally hired me

i think of those days
        not as the bad old days

but in the same way I think of
        a childhood friend i lost touch with

someone who would be a stranger now
        if we passed on the street"

MIKE JAMES

BASIL & SCOTCH

I know to pinch back the basil I planted
in the garden we made, in the soil that you tilled.
You crush the stems between your nails
below the buds, as I've shown you before
and before, that you pretend to forget
again and again.

We pile high the green harvest, wrapped
in the shirt you peeled off, the sun on your back.
You shoulder your way past
the wooden screen door, let it slap
on its frame, on its stiff metal hinges.

It's this simple, I say, through the whiskey
we drink in the dim of the kitchen. We smile, and we know
that basil and scotch will always be us.
But it's never that simple, no matter how much you drink.

And we've run around that block
before and again. We can only fool ourselves
for a little while now. For a little while,
at least, I can fool myself.

REBECCA JUNG

SCHOENBERG'S SECOND CONVERSION

When I was a young boy, they told me,
submerge your head in water, count to ten.
Instead I counted heartbeats and there were twelve
and I made my song.

I dreamed of Jacob's ladder,
angels flying upward, angels flying downward twelve rungs,
each a tribe, I thought, or perhaps a tone
and I wanted to raise my song.

There is one temple in heaven that only music opens
and for it I searched, dragging my twelve tribes of sound,
the modern Jacob, I thought, whose children are syllogisms
giving birth to law, giving birth to song.

Rung by rung, learning what I knew,
posing a problem, then solving and resolving,
then seeking a precept behind all solution
until I had climbed twelve rungs and prayed my song.

Now, fleeing Hitler in this month of fire,
I listen for the law of sound in the train's blunt rasp
and read of Jacob's dream and understand my blunder:
The ladder is beside him, but he does not climb.

When the train stops, it will be Paris
and I will disembark and find a ritual bath
and dunk myself a second time and, head submerged,
count heartbeats till twelve, and this time
the song will make me.

MARC JAMPOLE

ANDRENA ZAWINSKI
MISTY LAKE

PRAYER OF PULLING DOWN BRICKS

If you understand, things are just as they are.
If you do not understand, things are just as they are.

—Zen Saying

I.

One at a time, the hammer, the chisel, the chip
at the brick on the ladder one story up the half-
dismantled school, alone in the late April sun, hammering,
chipping, dropping, hammering, chipping, dropping,
he works

like a fieldhand digging potatoes, planting rice, picking
lettuce, possessed with the slow grace of timeless motion,
my perspective from the roadside atop the sloping space between us.

On the grass, bricks chipped, cleaned, stacked between the school
and an apple tree's craggy limbs beside a pillowy mock orange,
sweetening the breeze, muffling the chipping, chipping
or carrying it off, folded into its own waves—

His thoughts perhaps like these motions—
digging, picking, chipping, chanting, chipping, singing
quietly, folding into themselves like meditation.

Is this the prayer of pulling down bricks? The odd grace
of slow deconstruction as meditative action?

The old man rocks the ladder and climbs back up, chipping,
chipping again, and surely tomorrow, and the next day, and the next,
a holy approximation of a holy eternity—

II.

Yet isn't he the old plasterer I know
through my father, hammering
out a few more bucks
Social Security won't skim,
tongue fat with beer-thirst,
anxious for the tall-backed stool
at the Penn National where he will
not sweat under the stained ballcap
that now shields clouding eyes,

and he hopes his middle-aged daughter,
all cigarettes and jangling keys,
won't show, eyes hedging for money?

And what of the car repair place
beside the school, out of frame, where

the work is good but slow, and used
coolant and dirty oil seep down the steep
hillside across the road, downstream
from the township treatment plant?

Now comes a new meditation:
burnt oil singes the mock orange's scent,
a giant sewer stews below—
the frame stretches upon the image of an old man
alone, enraptured, chipping,
chipping a mantra, until it collapses with
an imaginary snap and crunch,

for you know however well he does it, what he does
is pull down bricks
to pay for closed-circuit ponies and beer
and his daughter who never grew up,
and the garage owner should be notified,
and likely a treatment plant is near anyplace
imaginable, and,
finally,

the craggy apple buds still,
and the mock orange is out sweetly,
the bricks are stacked like a pallet of neat dollars,
and in the April sun a solitary old man on a ladder
takes down an old school, brick by solid brick,
and there is something like grace to it,
nevertheless.

MIKE KANE

AARONEL deROY GRUBER
DREAM CITY

BENDING SCOOPING BENDING

there remains for us yesterday's street, always to revisit walking down
Rochambeau again.   going there a lot lately   this endless street
of my longings a cousin lived there but he had two parents and a sister   yet, yet
now it's a little different. I can hear music now   I could not hear   then

I'd not yet constructed the sound-rooms in my heart   the lengths & breaths
know the oboe can pierce my ribs without killing me   and I can hear the
rumbles, the groans and whispers of the lower strings as I bend on the wet street
scooping up discarded creamsicle wrappers if you send in enough you can
trade them for airplanes that almost fly or secret rings

or a magician's stock...masks of long-ago with gaping mouths & trap-door hats &
stacks of cards & wicked kings & queens I want to tell you of those that come
only in late day   when wild beasts roar among the fumes   when the sun
lingers   when I am tired   my eyes burn

I'm reading some poems of Rilke   a vacant street, my beloved
Rochambeau   when we got back to New York my parents quarreled again
everything so dismal I stood for lengths arching & gaping at bridges that
went on & on   no other side of rivers   my interminable street
remember that reaching down and scooping up   that gathering of voices

in orchestra again (how many years?) viola tucked under my chin   sky-god's
flutes & fiddles tumbling overhead & ashen halting basses below   a lone player
walks in the rain   to the edge of the city

past abandoned houses   bridges to the rim then   others come   horns
trumpets speak of beginnings   wide roads with their great trucks
roaring shaven bulls   lights breaking   no, no, I've not quite got it
please   today tired now bending scooping bending

* * *

so we pack up and move
        and there are new kids to fight

a new place to listen
      to the pounding on my face.

you're brave, one says
      and walks away.
I look up at vacant windows—
      hear the cars roll by.

***

      his body is a thou
sand sea squirms

don't forget
you

are asleep
and

and dream

ing loo
king between his thumb

and fore
finger is an eye

so fo
cussed that it is strange

all at once upon a time

ser
ious slaughter of the kind
beasts

hear ring a caco
phony of long

ings

***

the middle big room.
sit play airplane
inside flying ceiling
light off on off & on
momma runs tears
me up the floor
holds tight flies
outside! dark
porch moon lit
big street wet
big little cars
jump around no
people on the porch
others
who? don't see
faces

***

georgy she would yell out the open window *suppertime* & now it's always *david* my son's
name my father's name & now I slide back with her into the cool darkness of hickory and
pine & hold her aged head against my breast for a moment stroke it gently don't know how
it's been these last few days know she's been able to go to the grocery put some
coins dollar bills on the counter get bread get milk it's a pleasant drive along the belt
to ocean avenue where she lives alone but then when I get out of the car I stand for a moment
on the cement lot look around at the rectangular eyes that pass for windows & can feel the
darkness creep in slowly a kind of anesthetic to the soul climb the stairs slowly wait for a
moment before pushing the buzzer wait for the door to snap against the chain

***

a long dark wing inside

                                     a rapid space

family

             I never knew

                              old women

                         haggling

                                          over onions

lower limbs

        pipes

                   & tubes
              telescopic lens in her

                                        before

sleep &
      dream &
waking

roof flies

          open
sky startling
            blue

JOSEPH KARASEK

MARK ROBERTS
OAK AND IVY

MARK ROBERTS
CHURCH DOOR

MORNING MEDITATION

There are crimes being committed as I meditate.
Why do I meditate?

If only prayers were blooms like unto the lilac bush.

Yes, that is it, I will go somewhere peaceful today.
I remember Moraine State Park. I went there with a
lover. We took a blanket and sat by the shore. A Purple
Martin kept lighting near us, seemed to love us so. Like
an old soul in communion. Don't speak of the wearier
flesh here.

The waves lapped up and down.

And, then, we saw a lovely young woman and
a dog playing fetch in the water. The dog was so
tremendously happy and the sky so generous an
indigo, we could not help but look.

Then, the dog came out of the water with the stick
and, I saw it had but three legs.

I felt emotional pain at first. But, I asked the woman
why.

She answered there had been cancer, but the dog was
fine now. The dog regarded us happily as it shook
the water off.

She called the dog "Macy" and said, "If she is still happy
and ready to go on with life, I am ready to aid her in that."

I thought of Macy, and hope and meditation and
prayers and the lapping waters of a spiritual
body for the rest of that day.

I have stored it all within me and won't let go. I
will give the total reflection of it, the smile in
the eyes of a tiny Purple Martin, to you.

ROMELLA D. KITCHENS

ON PITTSBURGH AS POET'S CANVAS
(To Judith Vollmer)

Clear water from the north slips past the weathered hills, once spawned by sharp
upheavals. We are in need of cleansing. I am in Kittanning, watching a father

stand trial for murder. He starved his four year-old, shut her up in an attic—
Why must we spend time and money to defend such ordinary monsters?

Still, it is the right thing to do—you, of all people, understand. The Lenape, the "original
people," built their settlement by the great stream here, until we burned it down.

We looked for petroglyphs here, we looked for arrowheads & footprints, fire-cracked
rocks, shards, bottles with feathers inside them. We looked for red or sulfur-colored clay

drawings of bear, deer, we looked for any possible sign of people come before. I am
watching what look like giant crustaceans level the hillside near Springdale

for another shopping mall. What would Rachel Carson think? Trading in the old
woodlands.... Orange rust drips from soggy trees, junkyard cars, the hulking

headframes of abandoned coal mines. We are left with this overburden, all our
excesses, with our woodsheds falling over. Like you, I must bear witness:

Apollo, radioactive; all around me, the gray husks of steel mills, old slag heaps,
and in the midst of this long drawn-out goodbye, coal barges slowly chug upriver.

In taverns, millworkers drink with tombstone eyes, their children off to the promised land,
while we are left in this Old Country of obelisks, churches, thin black seams of coal:

*This morning I dreamed I was walking along a balustrade, Pittsburgh falling all around
me and no place for me to go.* Western Pennsylvania, the edge, the terminal moraine—

Roads and rivers here twist so sharply: eskers and drumlins, scoured by the water,
imbedded, exposed (why must we live in the geology of what remains?);

Industrial parks & shopping malls inside the grid of freeways sprout endless faceless
building, all cold geometry, all blocks and angles, with blank, fossil eyes.

You said, *Beginnings: the idea we stay in love with. I looked at the "new urbanism" photos...;
impossible to know if the streets are dead or living.* The Old Country still breathes...

This night at Oakmont, the river black anthracite. I watch it snake beside me from
the hillside as tiny, yellow truck lights glide across the bridge, like whispered prayers.

Below, other rivers that run beneath the city, hidden poems that probe & nourish,
that mourn the loss of landscape, called forward by the orbit of a very distant moon.

What is it that compels us to seek our own reflection? *A miner can't look out a window
for long, he has to go down.* We are all fossil fuel — Lenape canoes slip downstream.

NANCY L. KRZTON

DAN MOHAN
ADMIRING THE CUT

NATE SCHRITTER
GEORGE JONES

KATE SOFFEL WRITES TO HER HUSBAND FROM JAIL

On January 30, 1902, brothers Ed and Jack Biddle, both convicted of murder, escaped from the Allegheny County Jail in Pittsburgh, PA, with the help of saws and revolvers smuggled to them by warden Peter Soffel's wife Kate. She fled with the Biddles, one of whom had written love letters to her. The following afternoon both brothers were fatally shot by members of a sheriff's posse. Kate was wounded but lived to serve a prison sentence.

Dear Peter: It was not the silly stuff
I could have written better, not the praise
of two doomed brothers; well I know the ways
men purchase favors. No, I'd had enough
of being an appendix to your life
like some benign unnecessary growth
on your cold, clumsy flesh. I took an oath
that time should not speak lightly of your wife.

I heard the children, now no longer mine,
mouthing your priggish morals, heard them whine
our cheap complacent catechisms, saw
my future lost to joy and crushed in law
by men who know their beasts' and bankers' lives
far better than they ever know their wives.'

MARGARET MENAMIN

CHINA BLUE

Easter, you grace the Sanctuary, blue hydrangea,
mine to honor my father, not grieve a death.
After the service, only one drooping plant
remains, no justice to the man who conjures
brilliance from black earth and small seeds.
I take you home, douse with water.

Next day, like magic, you revive,
large, lush, bloom brightly into May,
when both my sisters call with news
of our father's death.

Time to dig a resting place,
add humus, water, tamp down.
Strong stems share the same root,
blossoms varied as daughters.

CHRISTINE DOREIAN MICHAELS

TRIUMPH

The bold eagle that you see

circling above my head

it's not a bird...

it's a burden of mine,

which grew wings and a body

to release the pain of my heart

with a great scream...

VIVIANA MIHELCIC

SANFORD N. ROBINSON, JR.
RUSHMORE, SEPT 11, 2001

BLESSINGS, CURSINGS: THE CHAINED SHELVES

I: The Dismantling

And the slab of the check-out counter with its oaken
Rivers worn in ancient grain, and the tilted shelves
Of penny candy and cigarettes, all empty behind it?
      Keep, keep, oh, God
      Keep it all nailed to the floor,
      Forever a bridge of hands,
      Bread, olives, soup, change, smiles,
      And sliced ham wrapped in white paper

Keep them keep them keep them all

And the aisles refusing to dull in darkness,
This endless counting of tile after tile
Into the lives that wore each step before me?
      Down, oh, up and down them all
      Into lives once and always
      Wish them to the pathways
      Between West Eighth and Oneida
      And the worlds behind front doors

Wish them wish them wish them all

II. Movers with Cigarettes

And the bare walls, exposed slats,
A disease to the touch, and this sliver under
The thumbnail of *Shit, shit, shit* echoing?
     Open, open, open like a wound
     For what's beyond this place,
     And damn the eyes of accusers
     Frozen open in knots of wood,
     Their faces in every inch of these walls

Damn the distances we now must go

And the movers grunting with Winstons dangling
Ashes to black boots with Cokes and dirty jokes,
And our shelving screaming then chained to a flatbed Ford?
     Curse, curse, curse them all
     With the tarot of my baseball cards,
     My best Mickey Mantle rubbed in hatred
     As those thieves back into our door
     And are gone to grinding gears up Eighth,

Where I run after, the *fuck-you's* bursting inside my lungs

And overhead, an abacus of blackbirds falls from the wires.

STEPHEN MURABITO

IN LOVE WITH THE B-GIRLS

I wanted the girl left at the bar just before
John Wayne and Susan Hayward lit up
Their cigarettes in *The Fighting Seabees.*

Again, Uncle Joe took us to the Saturday matinee,
Got us in for a buck, and said, "That John Wayne
Shoulda ran for president." My brothers nodded,

But I was mystified that the camera never returned to her,
Or never returned to the dark beauty leaving the hotel
Behind Robert Mitchum in *Cape Fear*, or never returned

To the woman who shook behind Elvis in *Viva Las Vegas.*
Where did they go when they left those clubs, or shot
Through those crossfire lobbies, or danced off the screen

Of another world while we neck strained around corners?
One by one, they arrived on cue across my bedroom ceiling
To float above the stories of mere actors and actresses:

Oh, my B-girls drank away the sorrows of this world,
Narrowly escaped their flesh-and-blood torments,
Danced themselves free from life's B-love affairs,

And lived in the celluloid behind my closed eyes.

STEPHEN MURABITO

PASTA

In college I loved Browning's phrase—
was it in "Two in the Campagna"?—
"tangled ropes of lasagna" and even today
I think it may have been pasta which
civilized the Italians so much they
refused to fight for Mussolini—remember how
Marshall Badoglio's armies surrendered in Africa
tutti and *rapidamente?*—and even the names
make you smile: orecchiette ("little lambs ears")
and orzo and penne and rigatoni and
of course gay bow-tie farfalle which
make me think of my favorite restaurant,
Flavio's, where the fat cook pounds his evil veal
but Nuncia is still beautiful and smiles as
she serves prawns and home-made fettuccine,
yes, and even surly Mencken called Puccini's music
"silver macaroni, exquisitely tangled"
and how lovely is "angel hair,"
semolina spun into a mist of pasta
that needs only some oil of the olive
and a few peppers or spring peas
to transport you to heaven and
whose preparation teaches
a great truth about cooking
and pleasure: focus, don't overdo it:
al dente, al dente.

ED OCHESTER

NATHAN SCHRITTER
DWAYNE DOLPHIN, SASSIE MARIES

NATHAN SCHRITTER
LOU STELLUTE

SHAKING HANDS WITH A JACKHAMMER

When you shake hands with a jackhammer
it's a grip you never forget.
You wake up, hands pinched & blistered,
ears throb to young Mick Jagger singing
SAT IS FACTION
& the hammer's your alarm clock;
it's seven a.m. & eighty-five degrees
& exhaust from the diesel compressor
smells sweet as women who pass your ditch,
skirts shorter than your imagination. When you're
eighteen and hammerin' foot-thick concrete
& blue stone for an hour, those long
legs are far away as double-time-and-a-half,
cold beer, Friday afternoon, but it's
Monday morning and Johnny Knee's been
drunk all weekend & says, "Even
Greta Garbo don't look good to me now!"
You're wonderin' who in hell is Greta Garbo.
Then Johnny cuts fruit into curlicues,
dumps it into the Igloo with ice
& it's over ninety now & the whole
ditch is thankful for the blessing
of Johnny's lemons.

When you shake hands with a jackhammer,
you hang on for dear life.
A ditch can kill a man, and old Adam,
who taught you the hammer,
he jumped down in the wrong ditch
lookin' busy for the boss
& the cave-in didn't cover his head
and intestines come out of his mouth.
They say your old man's
got cancer & high school buddies
from the team leave for college,
you're wonderin' if blistered
hands can fit a book spine & sink
a jump-shot again & you're hammerin' blue stone
& the Stones sing: "Can't get no
satisfaction..." & the hammer rings: "This,
this is all there is, Kid." The only thing left
is blowin' of Monday's dust with compressed air,
hearing the hiss & howl of the Ingersoll-Rand bleed down,
snaking hot, red hoses into tight piles for tomorrow.

WALT PETERSON

113

INTERMEZZO

When someone said Venice
She felt a rush across the back of her neck.
To be beautiful in a beautiful place.
To say the word piazza. To repeat it obsessively in her head
as she walked through the narrow arcades.
To lose herself in unfamiliar streets.
To enter the scarlet life of the city.

To watch. To do nothing quickly. To agree to be spellbound.

She was unafraid of excess, craved the sounds of fabrics,
tall shutters opening, the golden light of the basilica at noon.

The curve on curve of the arches became her second skin.

In the hour the lamps came on
she wondered what other lovers had used this room.

She was pulled as always to imminence and ruin.
She loved the excitement that it couldn't last,
the water lapping, the bells in her throat.

GRACE RISHELL

FERRIS CRANE

IN STILETTOS

Mostly I prance around in stilettos
to keep alive and inspired,

as if there were still such
things as Paris hats and seamed

stockings, which in fact I am told
are making a comeback.

I pretend to live in black &
white, and flirt with the likes

of men named Victor and Peter
or Pet-ah, as Bette Davis would

blot her lipstick and say. This is
how it once was, half-lidded and smoky,

perfumed with attar of vermouth, stirred
not shaken. The usual regrets were somehow

smoothed over with plans for cocktails
tomorrow, my dearest darling,

and haven't we been
married, truly, truly married?

Ah, the mysteries evoked by such
phrases: the man and woman stuff—

the desperate kisses, the blowing leaves,
the calendar pages torn away;

My tears are dim sparkles caught
by a loving camera, accompanied

by shades of a sweet tenor sax,
a melancholy throb—

delicious, actually.

JUDITH R. ROBINSON

TRANSLATING COLOR: A PRIMER

Living in corked-lined rooms, drinking lots of tea
and eating cakes with exquisite names like Madeleine
while waiting for a world to unfold... Marcel Proust,
with nerves so finely tuned, blamed potatoes
when, almost dead from his TB, he went
to the Jeu de Paume to see Vermeer's
VIEW OF DELFT, a picture he called
"the most beautiful in the world"—
and so moved he was by a patch of yellow
hidden on a tiny wall in this painting, that,
on the spot, he suffered a near-fatal stroke

A man who wrote *On Being Blue* chooses
to ignore the blue of blue jeans—and cells
that give salamanders their red spots
named *lipophores*—he is more interested
in medieval blues—the *woads*—but Proust,
had Proust seen the yellow of airport bulldozers,
rain slickers, or the flour stained by rat urine
on which Magellan's sailors subsisted
on their voyage around the world;
had Proust studied the inner cork of an egg
who is to say about any one thing's reception
in the world? maybe he, Proust, delicate and fine,
by seeing, would have been killed instantly

ROSALY DEMAIOS ROFFMAN

REBECCA WINTERS

TIME WARP

When I was young,
I wanted to be older.
Now that I am old,
I want to be younger.
There must have been
one day in the middle
when I was happy
with who I was.

I don't remember.

MICHAEL ROSE

DIANE R. ROSE
WOODEN DINGHY, VINEYARD HAVEN

GOOD FOLKS

(Gods of the ruins love their antiquities. The moon crackles.)

In Pennsylvania, where we live now is mostly farmlands.
Generally farm-owners are aged and empty-nesters.
Their sons and daughters went away
to bigger & better places.

Farm-owners still farm their lands
as best as they can. They stand beside unkempt barns,
wearing their farmers' hats,
chew tobacco and talk to each other
about weather forecasts, the price of gas.

If they see a car coming, they pause
expecting the driver to stop by. If someone's son
or daughter visits their parents with a newborn,
the whole neighborhood comes to greet the baby.
Then they baby talk, compare baby's features with their own.

After a long period of visitation,
they pretend to leave. The host asks them
to stay back for supper. They give ten reasons why
it is important for them to leave
but stay anyway.

The night deepens, the host starts a flame
for pig-roasting, takes out a cool cage
filled with chilled beer bottles. Someone brings out a guitar
from his truck and sings bluegrass.

Others gather around the flame and discuss
their childhoods, crack jokes about the kid who used to pee
on his bedroom floor, terrified of the bogeyman
hiding outside his window in the tree shadows.

SANKAR ROY

IN SEARCH OF MY NEW COUNTRY

I look for you in miasma
of the wild thicket. In the gentle tap
of my chisel, I peel through the walnut bark
to restore the lost face of you.

I smell cedar's warm, friendly scent
and inquire of an anonymous Arroyo,
your Ojibwa name. I explore
your Inuit face in the northern light

and look for your footprints
in soggy moss as I hear an iceberg moving,
opening the passage for caribous.
I seek your silhouette in the flickering fire,
a dog sleeping inside your tipi.

I watch the moon going down
into the deep of your chasm. I build a crown
of maple leaves, tint my face
in rooster blood. I scribble your map
in the wet ground and build your bust
using river mud.

I moan for your song
in the croon of night, alive
with crickets' drone and alligators' sigh.

SANKAR ROY

EVEN AT FIVE

I felt the shame
of running topless
in the rain.
It was the way
Eddie looked at me;
the way my small
nipples stiffened
when he gave me
his big tooth smile;
the way I ran
to hide in the alley
where I sat alone,
one arm wrapped
around my chest,
the other pulling
at the frayed elastic
on my cotton underwear.

JOANNE SAMRANEY

THE MESSENGER
—*for Art Blakey*

Born and raised among rivers,
he latched onto sticks, building
a signature crescendo that propelled him
eastbound beneath neon lights. For decades,
fearless men would contribute, magnifying
the sticks into rafts large enough to hold
a quintet comfortably. New and old waters mixed
until the first drops diluted, drowned in deaf echoes.
Living sounds would fade into memories of fractured voices
while the crescendo remained, crisp in cool-blue bottles.

DANIEL SHAPIRO

BREATH THROUGH BONES

Gracefully or not, I've arrived
at the age where lovely young women
feel fathered and safe
in my company, not knowing
how I ache for youth, how beauty
still intoxicates. And I love
this earnestness, like flame
beneath the skin of my daughter's face
as she counts time, waiting
to lift her flute, for lips
to form the embouchure — earnestness
that's part of me at this age
when she's the mouth of a long river
flowing into wordless song. Old friends
seem old, and my mother
can't go out in the cold at this age
when the insurance agent doesn't call
and husbands and wives are depressed
putting on weight and the Federal Reserve
says interest is down. Possibility
after possibility, like a mirage
you reach to touch, has disappeared
and slides around shimmering, a word
related to shimmy, the way an Egyptian
dancer moves her hips. My mind
moves like that at this age
and I think I'll be a child who wanders
lost in a dark forest whistling happily
because the cellos are touched with madness—
the slow movement of Beethoven's seventh.
Listen. Earth is turning, the sound
of breath through bones.

MIKE SCHNEIDER

PETER M. VERCILLA

from CHRISTMAS REQUIEM

Looking at the sky
we see a face, looking at the stars
we make stick-like constellations,
give them names. A game

perhaps like *Stewart Wins*, a whistling
and a hope. If it's the other way:
our face reflecting something about God,
it must be just a glimpse, a flicker,

an enigma, come to us
not in the clinking of a Bible verse,
but as a *saying*, underneath all this.
Forget what form, a word,

God in his fragile, blind, wind-battered world,
unrecognized. At the mirror, my sister's sure—
her bright red dress, the flowing robes she'll wear—
she'll be the center of the mass. Yet, making up herself,

she also makes the world. Grave with love,
she'll fold an altar cloth, she'll pass the wine.
People looking in her puffy eyes will see a kind
of enigmatic truth about themselves.

Woody Cone Flowers
poke above a winter flowerbed.
House sparrows stutter
between the air and ground,
squabbling for seed.
Little hulls of snow
speak themselves
out of an empty sky.
Upon a distant hill,
spidery black trunks of trees,
gray squall between, a delicate web
of branches dusted white.

****

Meanwhile, the decorations here
are all still up. The tattered foil
reflecting last, late sun. Neither the sun
center of a universe, nor the comic little stars

just switched on around this window.
A little dog yaps behind a chain-link fence—
somebody's limit, somebody's home—
certain that its bark is heard

throughout the neighborhood. It wears
a joke of a red wool jacket,
knitted for it by someone. *So, can you get in*
with just a Chihuahua? I'm saying yes.

RICHARD ST. JOHN

ROSE IN YOUR TEETH

Rose in your teeth, my darling, rose in your teeth,
and blood on your hands and shoes on your feet,
and barefoot in mud and how the shoes went floating
on bodies of water I sold them at Bakers and Burts
and carried the boxes on high; and there were women
galore who sat there in rows in their chairs on their thrones
in stockings of silk and we rolled by on wagons of wood,
and counted till midnight in codes and by numbers and letters
and I did the forms though once I led the charge
and I was the priest for two or three hours; and there were
forgotten styles in colors you couldn't imagine
and heels of the past and folded tongues and such,
and I was hungry at one in the morning and ate
forgotten foods and can't you tell how I
was a woman then and ransacked the upper shelves
and how I ran for the money and remembered
twelve to fourteen numbers and I knew
the stock and detested the manager and kept
my own tallies and ate my sandwich from a bag
during the later days of the war and just after,
when there were murder gardens everywhere.

GERALD STERN

BRANDON MCCHESNEY

ON GOBBLER'S KNOB

We gather on the hill outside Punxsutawney
to draw tight circles against the dark.

Five thousand strong, we twist and shout
to circulate blood to our frozen toes

then dance "The Pennsylvania Polka,"
bellow *Roll out the barrel* in the snow.

At six a.m. comet candles, flares, wheels of light
burst against the dark, and I think of Stonehenge

where Druid priests lit bonfires
against the endless nights.

Our hopes volley as
sizzlers salute the whistle pig

who whispers to the handler in his top hat:
"Six more weeks." Winter rules!

SHIRLEY S. STEVENS

FOOL MOON OVER THE MON

They sit on a bench near the bank of the mucky
river. Mid-July and the humidity so thick
you can see it swirling almost like mist.
The pollution is not bad tonight, not so bad, not
bad at all anymore now the mills shut down.
You can even see the moon and a few stars
rising out of the murky darkness, the night
almost indistinguishable from the water.

He puts his arm around her slenderness, the hand
damp with what had once been sweat cool against
her elbow. He finds her lips and the small plastic
clasp holding her bra together. She tries to pretend
this is not East McKeesport but France not
the Monongahela but the Seine, not this man
but another. Probably she will go through life
this way, enchanted, pretending, as if the moon
was not a three quarter moon, as if it were full.

CHRISTINE TELFER

LOST DOG

The neighbor girl calls out for her dog,
missing since last night, her voice echoing
its lamentation across the valley separating

her grief from ours. Mid-March, the sun
registers itself, as if the union
for which it operates has finally resolved

its endless negotiations with the clouds.
Sand-y, Sand-y, the girl sings its two note
rhythm. Ice thins into the pond's surface.

First robins. We lost one once:
I was just that neighbor girl's age: ten.
Blackie, her name. I'd be first to rise

so I could pet her all I wanted and still
she wanted more. Once she followed me
to school and the teacher gave us both

the rest of the day off. One evening
she didn't come home, just like that,
and after the search and the giving up,

I thought I saw her. Up all night, glued
to the window that overlooked the street,
the faint late dark indistinguishable

from the faint first light, she streaked,
a black blur, across the suburban lawns.
I woke my father but I still don't know

if it was her or if it was my heart shaped like her.
Now she approaches. *Have you seen her?*
Sandy? Face puffed, as if she'll never know

another night of complete sleep again.

PHILIP TERMAN

SLEEP

When, as a child, too early sent to bed,
The sun still golden in the evening sky,
Unwilling and protesting then went I,
Though sleep lay heavy on my weary head.
And in young womanhood, I loved the night:
Too sweet the dark, to sleep the time away!
To sing, to dance, to watch the stars till day—
This, to the youth, is glorious and right.
But sleep was not, and is not now, my friend:
For now, in age, sleep plays the fool with me;
O'erwhelms me in the busy afternoon,
But leaves me wakeful e'er the night doth end,
To wander in the garden restlessly,
And gaze, resentful, at the baleful moon.

ESTHER JACOBSON TUCKER

CHARLES FERRARO

PULLING A PIANO OUT OF THE POND

He always thrived on a project, especially when ordering
        everyone else around.
We bought the house with the intention of fixing it up,
        making it over, putting our

mark on it. By the following spring when the malignant cells
        were found all
the interior walls were torn down with only the support beams
        holding up the roof.

We bought a bolt of heavy upholstery fabric in a red
        and gold stripe. Cut it into
6-by-9 foot swaths to hang in for the missing walls.
        We'd mount one end to a dowel,

hang another from a beam and let it fall, no artful draping,
        no fringe, not even a finished
hem. It became our stage curtain, putting on little bits
        of scenes with an un-shaded

lamp as the spotlight. We played a family not necessarily happy
          but together (for now)
living around meals, work, treatment schedules, drywalling,
          board games, and his

medications. When he couldn't sleep he made notes/changes
          on the blueprints.
Moving closets, ripping out doorways. In the morning
          he'd have us knock down

our work from the day before and start again.
          It was as if we were pulling a piano
out of a pond, gaining a few feet to have sludge and wet grass
          drag it back into the murk.

With his new plans we could maybe get it out/finish the house,
          but the water logged keys and
mildewed frame made it worthless. We stopped asking
          if there was anything left worth saving.

BERNADETTE ULSAMER

FIELD NEAR RZESZOW

— family field originally passed through the line of women

How I had thought
this field, that meadow

is branded for eternity
            —H.D., "R.A.F." 1941

If these young rye flowers
stand up every summer
then fall under grindstones
& fists of bakers

if the stalks return to earth shorn & rough,
return green & moist every Spring,
            and if the ditches the aircraft wheels made

exist only in a censored photograph
            and in grass-tracings above tiny black *allées*
                        down where worms make their tracks

why am I standing on an open balcony
shouting for my own land,
            & hers before me?

                        Two men play guitars
down in the street on the edge of town
            and sing about the sky—

                        say, then shout, *niebo*
in a high laughing song, then
a woman's voice interrupts, in English,
            I see the back of her head

which looks tired, but she sounds intent,
we are all shouting

and I wish I knew Polish well enough
to hear the song again,

backstitch whose sky
        whose field, and who owns
the fernbanks across the field.

If I really owned my land
I would like to lie down on it through thirty seasons.

        Go into the woods
        get the black dirt
        for the flower pots.

        Save the brown water
        from the sinks & tubs,
        save the dregs of the soup pot
        for the geraniums,
        save the coffee grounds for the roses.

        For the best nightcrawlers
        dig under the shadows of boulders
        at the edge of the field where the table—
        rock piled with big rocks
        writes its story in long lines—

I would do these things.
I would study the scars
& glyphs the moraines clawed
in granite & limestone when the mammoth
plates scraped the land. When they stopped
moving they left overhangs & ledges,

& rock-niches for succulents and rock-rose.
        I get the hair on the back of the neck sensation
    at the edge of a field
                and like to read
& daydream in the green grass of a ditch
where grasses show
      the spitpockets inside their blades,
    and thatchings give groundcover
    to pebbles usually brown & black & sometimes a white
quartz fragment sits there reflecting
    light up onto the bird & butterfly paths.

Snakes, insect clouds & rabbits
    must like the heat of earth at that
        close range. And the tall blue

flowers rimming the deer beds—
        like hairlines,
    not much to go on, my field's wartime biography—

You could
walk across my field
    in ten minutes or less

and help me find out whether
the dragonfly visiting my wineglass
        lives in the grooves of the hawthorne or the
        cherry down in the little grove. I love

sky but not as much as wind on
                                tall grass that rustles all day.
Night lasts all night
while the field-spirits unseal
the photo of the field,

a simple field
stolen x-times over.
Unseal it and see:

the original wedding gift:
the furrows turned,
moist, open.

One word, *niebo,*
translates part of the song:

        If I say I like your *niebska* blouse
        I mean blue.
                        When I say
        the only *niebo* for me
        is the one above my family field
I am calling it heaven

JUDITH VOLLMER

GLASS CASE NO. 1: WANT

wrong wishes written on a rice grain	dirt from a burrow	Merriam's 315 damselfish* daredevil
failed wings of the dragonfly	the pebble she walked on for several miles	what follows the last bullet on her resume
slip of the potter-lover's hand	skeleton key	an "x" composed of eyelashes

LYNN WAGNER

BERT DINMAN
YOUNG DREAMS

WHAT I LIKED ABOUT HOME

Mama always called oatmeal
"mothers oats"
and cooked her hamburgers
a bit too hard
but navy beans she had down pat
yeah, navy beans she had down pat
        and that's what I liked about home

And we (almost) all got along
on the street(s) where I lived
of course, there were cousins
across the back way
and grandma across the front
And I don't remember nobody
speaking of fear
I just can't remember nobody
speaking of fear
        and that's what I liked about home

And Miss Feola
always smelled so fresh
and her house had to be
the cleanest in town
everything I needed
was in walking distance
and those streets
were just one big playground
Yeah, those streets were just
one big playground
and that's what I liked about home
I mean, I **really**
    liked this
        about home.

M.J. WASHINGTON

DIANE R. ROSE
UNE PORTE PROVENÇALE

THE MALADROIT

Is always there with a knife when you need a spoon.
Is always there with a basket instead of a pail.
Is always there like a star when you want a moon.
When you crave applause is folding her hands in prayer.

A knife may serve for eating the fragrant melon.
A basket dipped in the water swells and holds.
Unruffled, the lake on a clear night reflects a star.
Prayer can be sung, or the kind ear hear it as song.

But what can be done with the heart, the offered heart,
the maladroit, unwanted, idiot heart,
the panhandling slut on the street, with her lips in your face
closing and opening their vulgar red
unstoppable unforgivable "Bub, Bub, Bub"?

ARLENE WEINER

I SAT ON THE ROCK WITH MY SLEEVES ROLLED UP

He may be lying, he may not.
It's like trying to crack this rock with my hand.
What difference does the poplar tree make?
I sat on the rock with my sleeves rolled up.
A swallowtail dragging the ragged wing.
As if I didn't have a house to go home to,
a gray and white house, painted last summer.
As if something this solid should answer, as if
this stone ground smooth should be the solution.
He kept saying he loved me but that she
understood: a room wants a window on at least
two walls. He may be lying, he may not.
It's like trying to crack this rock with my hand.
I sat on the rock with my sleeves
rolled up. What difference does the poplar tree
make? As if I didn't have a house. A swallowtail
dragging. A gray and white house, painted
last summer. He kept saying he loved me
but that she understood. As if this stone ground
smooth. He may be lying. It's like cracking
a gray and white house. What difference
can a ragged tree make? He kept saying
that she understood about the room
and the window on at least two walls.

I sat on the rock with my sleeves rolled up.
Clouds kept moving, how could I
keep track of the wing?

LORI WILSON

PELL-MELL DUNE

On a bench of Barlovento,
slewing to a silky tune,
shifts a barchan pentimento
of a whispery simoom.

What nods just beyond the window
now expected to festoon?
Who lies hidden in the windrow?
Whose lies will the waves impugn?

These are thoughts we hadn't meant to
marmorealize in amber rune,
ambrotypes of sentimental
doings under summer moon.

Goes to show that 'what do we know?'
can't be said too much or soon—
reminiscences that startled
up that helter-skelter dune.

JACK WOLFORD

DAN MOHAN
RIVER VALVES

JOHN DEERE

I'm wearing this gold and green t-shirt.
John Deere   Moline, Illinois   est. 1837

I was born in Moline August 8, 1940.
My father worked for John Deere at the time.
He was an industrial engineer.

When I was a child my cousin Martha,
who was several years younger than I,
bit me on the nose.

When Katho and I went west
to Gothenburg Nebraska at Christmas 1982,
we stayed overnight in Moline.

We stayed overnight at an Econo Lodge
right across from a John Deere facility.

In the morning
we had breakfast at a Denny's
right beside the motel.
Outside the window we could see
a big billboard: John Deere.

When we got back on the road after breakfast,
I said to Katho,
"I think that was my cousin Martha
in the booth behind us at Denny's."

Katho said,
"Why didn't you speak to her?"

What would I have said?

MICHAEL WURSTER

THE WISP OF LIGHT

There is a sort of space
that's a different vastness

There is a heavenly body
that's a different great arch

Each cell in my body
is an unattainable distance

The unreachable constellations
find shelter in my flesh in my blood

Death, not to be denied
rises as it slowly falls

Life, not to be denied
Advances as it rushes away from us

Under the luminous sky over this world of dust
I grow old day after day

In the space beyond space
Alone, I blossom like a child.

HUANG XIANG

APRIL

There's no fool like her,
   spinning
last leaf-fall's remnants against
    her sprouting shoots,
poking her tender bulb-tips through
    old debris, and thinning
left-behind snowpiles crusted
    with icy soot.

None fickle as April
   on Monday
all sun and smiles—and then
    blowing
shoulders cold long before weekend;
    by Sunday
sodden with persistent tears—
    or else snowing,

beating with stinging pellets
    her pastel crocus.
It's true that a lady, with whimsy,
    may change her mind,
but April rides the revolving door,
    out of focus,
coquettish, tumultuous, maudlin
    and unrefined.

There's one born every minute;
                we're sucked in
by the mad maiden's bouquet
                of pink and yellow
hazing the skeletons of trees.
I forgive her every year, made sentimental,
                mellow
despite her raving, ravished by blossom—
                perfumed breeze.

"Babbling and strewing" or—presto!—wild
                gusting and soaking,
dimming red tulips in mist to
                grey and moody,
this magic green spell, for all that
                she's provoking,
flips from her sleeve a spray of short-lived
                beauty.

JUDY YOGMAN

TWILIGHT INNINGS

PNC Park April 15, 2003

As 8 o'clock steals over the grandstand, hooking 'round
the steel spine towers, the polished lights take hold of the field,
popping awake the players, white sleeveless jerseys over rolled
black arms and high stirrups, the iron grate grain of the grass,
the shine of the plate and snapping flag, all stand an inch
closer to reality like a Forbes Field photo's event horizon, all an inch
farther into time, into my grandfather's barnstorming, my father's
unassisted triple play, my hours trying to catch like Clemente,
all together, today and the past, under a sherbet moon,
and the organist plays us all a jig.

MICHAEL W. YOUNG

RUTH ELLA HENDRICKS

DRIVING THE LAURELS

Somerset, PA in the Laurel Mts.

"all the bright clouds and clusters,
beasts and heroes,
glittering singers and isolated thinkers
at pasture."
— from Gerald Stern's *Cow Worship*

Driving the Laurels, I wind the regular route to a week of work
before leaving one coast behind for another, Pennsylvania
greening past Somerset. Driving this road where the deer leapt
and fell, legs tucked under, head forest bent, as if to have tried
a last time to lift itself up for one more look back, I drive
these mountains laden with words to fill classrooms I inhabit
in this string of last days east, in my hands these gifts:

Kenyon's peonies and Sandburg's fog, some of Harjo's horses,
one tidy wheelbarrow from Williams. Driving the Laurels past
a store that says *Open* that never is, a roadside sign peddling
gravel and clean fill instead of corn, detour roping an Elks Hall
and Amish draped in black behind bare windows, I drive fast
trying to catch some AM news above the static between hills,
past the silo a funnel cloud lifted last year then dropped down.

I drive fast past willows at the pond's edge, past forsythia
in the patches, johnny jumpups nosing through the berm. I work
the week in rural America, cut my way through untamed flowers
to coax from children a long look at what they hold here:
these cows at pasture their udders fat and heavy with what
we need, and those spring peepers—the high-pitched chorus
they will bring when night rolls down to greet the creek grass.

ANDRENA ZAWINSKI

ANDRENA ZAWINSKI
WATER CHI

ENDYMION ABDICATING ETERNAL YOUTH WHICH AT EIGHTEEN METRES BECOMES THE PORTRAIT OF MY FATHER IN A HOSPITAL BED (HOMAGE TO DALI)

last day on loan from summer
before the loaming of
autumn

bathroom window closed before
showering

wisdom of washing my sweaters
last friday apparent
this friday

thoughts of

money work or loved ones
are vexations

but so are

enlightenment wisdom or
buddhahood

fear verging on excitement

astronomers have discovered an invisible galaxy
mostly made of dark matter
which
makes up about 23% of the universe

stuff of stars planets people contribute 4%
the rest of the universe is driven by an even more
mysterious
thing called

dark energy

the owner of the indianapolis colts
jim orsay
bought the manuscript of
on the road
for $2.43 million
the end of the 120 foot scroll eaten by a dog

in italy
it
was read nonstop

currently
its on its way to
las vegas

the welkin
cipolin

the myths are meaningless
until one sees

endymion

abdicating the
promissory of youth
aeons ago

in a hospital bed
dreaming in the gloam

VINCENT ZEPP

BERLIN MEMOR
FORECLOSED HOTEL

CARSON ST. EPIPHANY

There's something beautiful
about this old woman waiting for the bus,
she's wearing a brightly colored floral dress,
she's even got flowers on her blue canvas shoes.
She's at least 70 years old,
she's in full bloom on the cement sidewalk,
her legs are like stems,
her flowered dress moves in the breeze,
she is the essence of cool
with her sunglasses and gray hair.
She's grinning as the bus arrives,
she just knows that someone is writing a poem about her.
She gets on the bus
and Death is the driver,
and Death just has to grin
and admire that dress,
she smiles back,
they nod to each other,
she takes a seat with the other souls,
the light turns green,
the bus pulls away
and she's gone, gone, gone ...

BOB ZILLER

Contributor Notes

KATHERINE AYRES is the author of ten books for children. Her short story credits include *Cricket, Spider, Ladybug, Pockets* and *Children's Writer*. Her newest picture book is *Up, Down and Around*. She teaches writing to graduate students at Chatham University.

MARILYN BATES is author of the poetry collection, *It Could Drive You Crazy*. Her work has appeared in *Poet Lore, The Potomac Review, One Trick Pony, The Patterson Literary Review, The Birmingham Poetry Review*.

JOAN E. BAUER's poems have appeared in *Blue Arc West: An Anthology of California Poets, The Comstock Review, 5 AM, Main Street Rag, Poet Lore, Quarterly West*. She was associate editor of *Only the Sea Keeps: Poetry of the Tsunami*, Bayeux Arts, 2005.

CLAIRE BAUERLE graduated from Carnegie Mellon and earned her M.A. in creative writing at Johns Hopkins. Since then, her work has included teaching in community college, brochure writing, communication design, technical editing.

RUTHANNE F. BAUERLE is a member of the Associated Artists of Pittsburgh and owner of Fox Chapel Images, LLC. Her images of distressed items and nature from diverse geographic locations are rich in texture and capture the extraordinary amid the ordinary.

JAN BEATTY's new book, *Red Sugar*, will be published by the University of Pittsburgh Press in Spring, 2008. Other books include *Boneshaker, Mad River*, and *Ravenous*. Beatty directs the creative writing program at Carlow University.

PETER BLAIR's most recent book of poems is *The Divine Salt*, published by Autumn House Press, 2003. He is a native of Pittsburgh now living in North Carolina where he teaches at the University of North Carolina, at Charlotte.

ANITA GEVAUDAN BYERLY is the author of *Digging a Hole to China*, 2001, and *October Light*, 2008, chapbooks. Her work has appeared in *5 AM, The Ledge, Pittsburgh Post-Gazette, Pittsburgh Quarterly, Loyalhanna Review, Earth's Daughters, Sandburg-Livesay Anthologies, yawp*, www.poetrymagazine.com and www.poetrypoetry.net.

RICK CAMPBELL's newest book is *Dixmont*, Autumn House Press. His other books are *The Traveler's Companion*, Black Bay Books, 2004, and *Setting The World In Order*, Texas Tech, 2001. He teaches English at Florida A&M University in Tallahassee, Florida.

JAY CARSON teaches creative writing, literature, and rhetoric at Robert Morris University. His work has appeared in *Paper Street, The Louisville Review, Mudfish, Willard and Maple, Limestone*, and *Southern Indiana Review*.

ANNABELLE CLIPPINGER is Director of PITT ARTS. She has published *Sky Frame*, 2000, and *Cloud Banner*, 2002, both by Potes & Poets Press. She is an instructor of English at the University of Pittsburgh.

HAZEL COPE was raised in England which was good preparation for living among Pittsburgh's lovely hills, rivers, people and history.

FERRIS CRANE is a photographer living in Pittsburgh.

JOHN R. CUNNINGHAM holds an MFA in Writing from the University of Pittsburgh. His work has appeared in *Proteus, The Insatiable Pimento, Pittsburgh Post-Gazette, City Paper*, and *Cafe Magazine.*

ANN CURRAN is the author of *Placement Test.* She is a contributing editor of *Pittsburgh Magazine.* Her poetry has appeared in *Commonweal, Loyalhanna Review, Pittsburgh Post-Gazette, Three Rivers Poetry Journal* and *Writers Digest.*

JAMES DEAHL was born in Pittsburgh in 1945. He moved to Canada in 1970. He is the author (or, in the case of Tu Fu, translator) of sixteen literary titles including *The River's Stone Roots: Two Dozen Poems by Tu Fu* and *When Rivers Speak.*

TOI DERRICOTTE is the author of *The Black Notebooks*, 1997, *Tender*, 1997, *Captivity*, 1989, *Natural Birth*, 1983 and 2000, and *Empress of the Death House*, 1978. She has received two Pushcart Prizes, 1989 and 1998. Her essay, *Beginning Dialogues*, appears in *The Best American Essays of 2006.* She is professor of English at the University of Pittsburgh.

ANNETTE DIETZ's poetry has appeared in *Paper Street.* She is an award-winning painter, member of the Pittsburgh's Society of Artists and Pittsburgh Poetry Exchange.

BERT DINMAN is a physician, a Professor (University of Michigan, Ohio State University, 1957-72 and University of Pittsburgh, 1987-2005) and a photographer. He has exhibited with the Associated Artists of Pittsburgh, 2006, and at the Carnegie Library, 2007.

PATRICIA DOBLER (1939—2004) was born Patricia Averdick in Middletown, Ohio. Her book, *Talking to Strangers*, was winner of the Brittingham Prize in Poetry from the University of Wisconsin, 1986. She taught at Carlow University and directed its Women's Creative Writing Center until her death. Dobler also led Carlow's writing workshop, Madwomen in the Attic.

BARBARA EDELMAN is currently a Visiting Lecturer in English at the University of Pittsburgh. Her book is *A Girl in Water*, Parallel Press, 2002, and she appears in two anthologies, *A Fine Excess: Contemporary Language at Play*, Sarabande Books and *Encore: More From Parallel Press Poets*, Parallel Press.

ZIGGY EDWARDS is a first-generation Pittsburgher who earned a degree in fiction writing at the University of Pittsburgh. Some of Ziggy's poems have appeared in *Ship of Fools, Nexus, Main Street Rag, Confluence* and *Paper Street.*

SUE SANIEL ELKIND (1913-1994) was a lifelong resident of Pittsburgh. She published five collections—*No Longer Afraid*, 1985, *Waiting for Order*, 1988, *Another Language*, 1988, *Dinosaurs and Grandparents*, 1988, and *Bare As The Trees*, 1992. She founded and ran the Squirrel Hill Poetry Workshop in Pittsburgh.

TIMONS ESAIAS' fiction has appeared in fourteen languages, and his poetry has been translated into Spanish, Swedish and Chinese. His poetry chapbook, *The Influence of Pigeons on Architecture*, is in its second edition. He is Adjunct Faculty at Seton Hill University, in the Writing Popular Fiction M.A. Program.

RINA FERRARELLI's work, poetry and translation, has been collected in five books. She has been published in *Artful Dodge, Barrow Street, The Chariton Review, Chelsea, College English, 5 AM, The Kansas Quarterly, Laurel Review, The Pittsburgh Post-Gazette, Poet Lore, Runes, Tar River Poetry, VIA, Zone 3.*

CHARLES FERRARO is a graduate of Point Park University, 2003, with a B.F.A. in Photography. He works in both photojournalism and commercial photography. His work was published in The Best College Photography Annual, 2002.

GAIL GHAI, a former Pittsburgher, teaches at Sarasota High School in Florida. Recent work has appeared in *Kaliope, Florida English, Pittsburgh Post-Gazette* and *The Comstock Review*. She is the author of *Painted Words*, a color thesaurus poster: www.artpoetica.com.

JACK GILBERT was born in Pittsburgh in 1925 and published four volumes of poetry: *View of Jeopardy*, 1962, winner of the Yale Younger Poets Series, *Monolithos*, 1982, a finalist for the Pulitzer Prize, *The Great Fires*, 1994, and *Refusing Heaven*, 2005, winner of the National Books Critics Circle Award and the Los Angeles Times Book Prize.

LOIS I. GREENBERG's work has appeared in *Paper Street*, the *Pittsburgh Post-Gazette, HEArt, The National Book Foundation Anthology, The Eternal Fire*, on e-zines *hotmetalpress* and *writersalliance.*

AARONEL deROY GRUBER is an artist currently using both traditional photographic techniques and digital technology. Honors include Carnegie Museum of Art's 1997 exhibition, *Pittsburgh: Photographs Since 1850*. In May 2005, she received a purchase award from the 100 Friends of Art from the Associated Artists of Pittsburgh.

GRACE GUNDERMAN taught senior high school English for twenty five years at Gateway High School. She is the mother of two daughters who are as different as sun and shadow.

BEN HARTLEDGE was the recipient of the 2007 Baum Grove Award. His poems have appeared in *Naropa, Beaux Arts, Tele-art.com*. Ben is an MFA candidate in Poetry at Bennington College.

TIM HEMPFIELD is a local poet who used to specialize in dark poems with a humorous twist. His money comes from loafing in a store at night until he can get a real job.

RUTH ELLA HENDRICKS' film, *Quart Jar Poet*, featuring the poet Dorothy Holley, premiered in 2005. Her publications include the *Pittsburgh Post-Gazette, City Paper* and anthologized in *After the Bell: Contemporary American Prose about School*, University of Iowa Press and *Voices from the Attic Volume XIII*, The Carlow University Press.

DOROTHY HOLLEY combined three interests: gardening, poetry and photography in her latest book, *The Garden Journals,* published by FootHills Publishing, 2006. FootHills published *A Whole Quart Jar,* 2005.

MIKE JAMES is the author of *Not Here*, Green Bean Press, 2000, *All Those Goodbyes*, Talent House Press, 2001, *Pennies From An Empty Jar,* Another Thing Press, 2002, and *Nothing But Love*, Pathwise Press, 2004. His most recent publication is *Alternate Endings*, FootHills Publishing, 2007.

MARC JAMPOLE is the author of *Music from Words*, 2007, Bellday Books, Inc. His publications include *Mississippi Review, Oxford Review, Janus Head, Main Street Rag, Ellipsis*.

REBECCA JUNG's publications include *The Pennsylvania Review, Impetus, The Pittsburgh Quarterly, Wazee-Journal, MiPo, The Pittsburgh Post-Gazette, The Burning Word, CC&D, The Festival of Voices Anthology, Three Rivers Art Festival: The Boat as Metaphor*, and a chapbook titled *The Relic Maker*.

BRIAN KALDORF is a Pittsburgh based photographer. His photographs create a fresh and lively feel through the use of color, form, and perspective. Through the genres of food, still life, and fashion photography, Brian's images convey a rich, cohesive vision, recognizable in the manner he interprets color.

MIKE KANE lives in Johnstown and is executive director of a community foundation. His poems have appeared in a number of publications, and he has published a chapbook, *Gathering Place*.

JOSEPH KARASEK is a former violist with the National Orchestral Association. He's taught Music at Long Island University and James Joyce's *Ulysses* at the Academy for Lifelong Learning at Carnegie Mellon University. His publications include *The Pittsburgh Post-Gazette, The Exchange, Yawp, The Pittsburgh Quarterly, Paper Street, Janus Head, Blue Arc West*, Tebot Bach, 2006, and *Only the Sea Keeps: Poetry of the Tsunami*, Bayeux Arts, 2005.

ROMELLA KITCHENS is a writer and performance artist. Her poems have appeared in *Essence Magazine, 5 AM, Van Gogh's Ear*. A first chapbook, *Hip Hop Warrior*, was published by Main Street Rag in 2005. Two more chapbooks are forthcoming from Pudding House Press.

NANCY KRZTON spent her childhood years in Greece, Turkey and Germany. After graduating from Allegheny College, she practiced journalism and law.

ANDREA LONDON has been photographing faces in her Pittsburgh, Pennsylvania, studio for nineteen years. She is known for her privately-commissioned black & white fine art portraits, and her stock photography is licensed throughout the world.

BRANDON McCHESNEY grew up in the rural hills of Pennsylvania. His photographs are influenced by internal family strife, the rough, dirty graininess of dirt-poor farm life and his years as a volunteer firefighter. Brandon received his B.S. in 2005. Currently, he owns a photography company in Pittsburgh.

BERLIN MEMOR is a photographer from Pittsburgh.

MARGARET MENAMIN wrote her first poem when she was in the second grade and was published in *Seventeen* before she was 20. Her poems have appeared in *Good Housekeeping, The Missouri Conservationist, The Lyric, The Formalist, Iambs and Trochees*, and *The Pittsburgh Post-Gazette*. Her book is *Sonnets for a Second Summer*, Westphalia Press, 1996.

CHRISTINE DOREIAN MICHAELS came to Pittsburgh from England in 1971. Her publications include *Taproot, Pittsburgh And Tri-State Area Poets, The Exchange, No Choice But To Trust, The*

Sandburg-Livesay Award, Signatures, The Pittsburgh Post-Gazette and *Only The Sea Keeps: Poetry of the Tsunami,* Bayeux Arts, 2005.

VIVIANA MIHELCIC was born in Sighisoara-Transylvania, Romania. She came to the U.S. in 1995. She is a member of the International Society of Poets, 2006-2007.

DAN MOHAN graduated from Point Park College. In 2003, Dan established *Dan Mohan Photographs,* creating images for healthcare, education and corporate brochures.

STEPHEN MURABITO is an associate professor of English at the University of Pittsburgh at Greensburg. His short stories have appeared in *North American Review, Antietam Review, Brooklyn Review,* and *Paper Street.* His chapbook is *A Little Dinner Music,* Parallel Press, 2004. *The Oswego Fugues,* 2005 and *Communion of Asiago,* 2006, were both published by Star Cloud Press.

ED OCHESTER has been editor of the Pitt Poetry Series since 1978. He is former director of the creative writing program at the University of Pittsburgh, and is professor emeritus of English there. He is the author of over fourteen volumes of poetry, the newest being *Unreconstructed: Poems Selected and New,* Autumn House, 2007.

WALT PETERSON is affiliated with the International Poetry Forum and the Pennsylvania Council on the Arts, and does writing workshops at Pine Grove State Correctional Institute and with the Sisters of Saint Francis. His chapbook, *In the Waiting Room of the Speedy Muffler King,* was published by Unfinished Monument Press, 1999.

LAURA PETRILLA is a graduate of the Art Institute of Pittsburgh and a freelance photographer, whose work appears in both publications and advertisements. A member of the Associated Artists of Pittsburgh, she's exhibited in Pittsburgh galleries, including the Carnegie Museum.

GRACE RISHELL is a former newspaper reporter and member of the Madwomen in the Attic poetry workshop. She is also a member of the board of associates of the International Poetry Forum. She lives in Sewickley, PA.

MARK ROBERTS is a photographer and writer born in Hemal Hempstead, England, currently living in Pittsburgh. He works in 35mm-format, digital and medium format film. He currently teaches full time at Youngstown State University. www.robertstech.com.

JUDITH R. ROBINSON was editor of *Living Inland,* 1989, Bennington Press; wrote *The Beautiful Wife and Other Stories,* 1996, Aegina Press; poetry editor of *Signatures,* 2001, 2003, and 2006, Ring Road Press. She was editor of *Only the Sea Keeps: Poetry of the Tsunami,* 2005, Rupa Publishers, Inc. and Bayeux Arts.

SANFORD N. ROBINSON JR. was born, raised and educated in Pittsburgh. He came to photography through a fondness for travel and adventure. His favorite photography subjects are nature/ landscapes and urban images.

ROSALY DEMAIOS ROFFMAN teaches at Indiana University of PA. She is the co-editor of *Life on the Line,* three chapbooks and *In the Fall of A Sparrow.* Publications include *MacGuffin, Zone 3,*

Centennial Review, Pittsburgh Quarterly and *Only The Sea Keeps*, Bayeux Arts, 2005. She is facilitator of the Squirrel Hill Poetry Workshop and was twice nominated for a Pushcart Award.

DIANE R. ROSE came to photography through a love of travel, nature, and off-the-beaten path experiences. Her work shows a love of lighting, color, shapes and patterns—either man-made or naturally occurring—often near water. www.dianerose.com.

MICHAEL ROSE earned both his Bachelor's and Master's degrees in Metallurgical Engineering from Rensselaer Polytechnic Institute. His poetry explores relationships, values, the interface between man and nature, and modern politics. His publication credits include *Signatures* and *Rensselaer.*

MICHAEL D. ROSELLA was born in Pittsburgh in 1933. He is a graduate of University of Pittsburgh's School of Dental Medicine, 1957. His previous exhibits include *Pittsburgh Streets 1950s* and *Last Day of Dixmont*, both shown at Silver Eye Center for Photography.

SANKAR ROY is a winner of PEN USA Emerging Voices, author of three chapbooks—*Moon Country*, 2006, *The House My Father Could Not Build,* 2007 and *Mantra of the Born-free*, 2007, all by Pudding House. He was an associate editor of *Only the Sea Keeps: Poetry of the Tsunami*, Rupa Publication, India and Bayeux Arts, Canada. His poems have appeared in over forty literary journals. He created www.writersalliance.net and Poets for Humanity (www.poetsforhumanity.com).

JOANNE SAMRANEY is author of the poetry chapbook, *Grounded Angels*, 2001, Acorn-Rukeyser Award Winner. Her work has appeared in *The Panhandler, Verve, Voices in Italian Americana* and *Main Street Rag.*

MIKE SCHNEIDER is a science writer at Carnegie Mellon. His poems have appeared in *5 AM, Paper Street, Poet Lore, Shenandoah* and *Poetry*. His chapbook, *Rooster,* was a runner-up in the 2004 Main Street Rag chapbook competition.

NATE SCHRITTER first encountered the Pittsburgh jazz scene while earning his degree from the Art Institute. A chance meeting with local jazz great Dwayne Dolphin in the summer of 2005 sparked his current project, an ongoing documentation of Pittsburgh jazz musicians on and off stage.

DANIEL M. SHAPIRO is a high-school teacher and graduate student at the University of Pittsburgh. His work has appeared in *The Pedestal, Oyez Review, American Drivel Review,* and *Tattoo Highway*. His chapbook is *Teeth Underneath*, Foothills Publishing.

GERALD STERN was born in Pittsburgh in 1925. His most recent book is *Everything Is Burning,* Norton, 2005. His many honors include The National Book Award, 1998, and election as Chancellor of The Academy of American Poets in 2006. He taught at the University of Iowa Writers' Workshop.

SHIRLEY S. STEVENS, a member of the Squirrel Hill Poetry Workshop and Pittsburgh Poetry Society, is poetry columnist of *The Upper Case*. Her work has appeared in *City Paper, Common Wealth, Poet Lore* and *The Christian Century.*

RICHARD ST. JOHN's first book, *The Pure Inconstancy of Grace*, was published in 2005, Truman State University Press. His poems have appeared in *Carolina Quarterly, Poet Lore, Sewanee Review* and include a nomination for a Pushcart Prize by *HEArt*.

PHILIP TERMAN's books include *Rabbis of the Air*, Autumn House Press, 2007, *Book of the Unbroken Days*, 2005, and *The House of Sages*, 1998, both Mammoth. His poems have appeared in *Georgia Review, Poetry, Kenyon Review, Gettysburg Review*, and *Blood to Remember: American Poets Respond to the Holocaust*.

CHRISTINE TELFER is former editor of *The Exchange*. Poetry credits include *The Pittsburgh Quarterly, The Pittsburgh Post-Gazette, Rain City Review, Main Street Rag, The Oakland Review Anthology* and *Whisky Island*.

ESTHER JACOBSON TUCKER for 25 years operated The Tuckers, an antiquarian bookstore in Squirrel Hill. She has been published in *Giants in the Earth*, East Lansing, 1991, *Renaissance Magazine* and the *Pittsburgh Post-Gazette*.

BERNADETTE ULSAMER earned a BA in Poetry and a MLIS from the University of Pittsburgh. Publishing credits include *Pittsburgh City Paper, The Main Street Rag*, the anthology *Voices from the Attic*, and two self-published chapbooks, *Blue Notebooks* and *The Strangest Thing I've Ever Seen*.

PETER M. VERCILLA was born in New Castle and has lived in Pittsburgh since 1983. He's had a lifelong passion for the natural world, art and architecture. His study of biology and clinical medicine have given him both a micro and macroscopic view of our natural and built world.

JUDITH VOLLMER is professor of English and Creative Writing at the University of Pittsburgh, Greensburg. She is co-editor of the poetry journal *5 AM*. Her books are *Level Green, Black Butterfly, The Door Open to the Fire*, and, most recently, *Reactor*.

LYNN WAGNER has poems in *Subtropics, Shenandoah, Chautauqua Literary Review*, and *5AM*. Lynn received an MFA from the University of Pittsburgh, where she was awarded the Academy of American Poets prize in 2002.

M.J. WASHINGTON grew up in Braddock, PA. Her documentary, *To Dance is to Live!*, highlights the life of African-American ballerina, Janet Collins. In 2004, Washington founded the Under Authority Theatre Group which sheds light on the lives of African-American women.

ARLENE WEINER is the author of *Escape Velocity* (Ragged Sky, 2006). She has had poems published in *Pleiades, Poet Lore, The Louisville Review*, and *US 1 Worksheets*, and read by Garrison Keillor on his *Writer's Almanac*.

REBECCA WINTERS is a photographer from Pittsburgh.

LORI WILSON has taught economics at San Francisco and San Jose State Universities. Her work has appeared in *5 AM, The Comstock Review, Main Street Rag, Paper Street*, and *Southern Poetry Review*.

JACK WOLFORD passed away December 16, 2005. He was loved for his humor, his irascibility, and his loyalty to poetry. Jack was a member of Pittsburgh Poetry Exchange and an assistant editor at Autumn House Press.

MICHAEL WURSTER is a founder of Pittsburgh Poetry Exchange and teaches at Pittsburgh Center for the Arts School. In 1996, he was an inaugural recipient of a *Pittsburgh Magazine* Harry Schwalb Excellence in the Arts Award for his contributions to poetry and the community.

HUANG XIANG is a poet/calligrapher. He was born in China in 1941. He began writing in the 1950s, was tortured for his writing and for his advocacy of human rights. In exile in the U.S. since 1997, he was first resident poet in Pittsburgh under Cities of Refuge North America program for writers in 2004-2006.

JUDY YOGMAN's poems have appeared in *Taproot, Thirteen, Poetalk Magazines*, and *The Forum*, and have been anthologized in *Crossing Limits* and *Out of the Rough*.

MICHAEL W. YOUNG teaches at La Roche College in Pittsburgh. He is the winner of teaching awards at two universities and twice included in *Who's Who Among America's Teachers*. His work has appeared in *Cottonwood, The Storyteller, Nebraska Magazine*, and *A Hero Bourne*.

ANDRENA ZAWINSKI's most recent publications include *The Progressive Magazine, Psychological Perspectives Journal of Jungian Thought, Many Mountains Moving, Comstock Review, CQ, San Francisco Reader, Monterey Poetry Review*.

VINCENT ZEPP has served as Poetry Director for the Three Rivers Arts Festival and Director of the Fourth River Poetry Festival. His work has appeared in *The Exchange, Membrane Envelope, The Pittsburgh Post-Gazette, City Paper*, and poetrymagazine.com.

BOB ZILLER's work has appeared in *The American Association of Haikuists Newsletter, Brain Wash, even, Further, Manna, Mean Zine, The New People, Our Wonderful Culture*, and *Transmission*. His books include: *Translated from the Night* by Jean-Joseph Rabearivelo (as translator), *Azure Plough*, and *Van Gogh Surfing*.

Acknowledgements

CLAIRE BAUERLE: a version of "Skunk Cabbage" originally appeared in *Great Stream Review* and subsequently in a limited edition chapbook, *A Poetry Sketchbook*, Paper Pagoda Press. JAN BEATTY: "Pittsburgh Poem" first appeared in *Mad River*, U of Pgh Press; "Going Deep for Jesus" first appeared in *Boneshaker*, U of Pgh Press. PETER BLAIR: "Friday for the River" was previously published in *The Divine Salt*, Autumn House Press, 2003. Reprinted by permission of the publisher. ANITA GEVAUDAN BYERLY: "Braddock Avenue" was first published in the Sandburg-Livesay Award Anthology, *No Choice but to Trust*, 2000; subsequently in *poetrymagazine.com*, 2001 and the poet's chapbook, *Digging a Hole to China*, 2001. "Steam Rising" was first published in *The Ledge*, 1995; subsequently in the Sanburg-Livesay Award Anthology, *No Choice but to Trust*, 2000, and the poet's chapbook *Digging a Hole to China*, 2001. RICK CAMPBELL: "The Candles at Margaret Mary Catholic Church" and "How the Streets in Front of Kaufmann's Department Store Tell Me I Am Home" appeared in *Setting The World In Order*, Texas Tech University Press, 2001. JAY CARSON: "Baking the Ginger Boy's Tongue" first appeared in *Euphony*, University of Chicago, Summer 2004. HAZEL COPE: "July 12, 1904" was first published in *Signatures*, 2006, Carnegie Mellon and Ring Road Press. TOI DERRICOTTE: "Before Making Love" and "On Stopping Late in the Afternoon for Steamed Dumplings" first appeared in *Captivity*, 1989. PATRICIA DOBLER: "Effigy" and "Juarez, 1978" was previously published in *Living Inland*, Bennington Press, 1989 and in *Collected Works of Patricia Dobler*, Autumn House Press, 2005. Reprinted by permission of the executors of the estate of Patricia Dobler. ZIGGY EDWARDS: "Hope's White Shoes" orginally appeared in her chapbook *Hope's White Shoes*, Pittsburgh Poetry Exchange. SUE SANIEL ELKIND: "Jerusalem of My Dream" previously appeared in *Living Inland*, Bennington Press, 1989. Reprinted by permission of executor of estate of Sue Saniel Elkind. TIMONS ESAIAS: "Would I Give the World, All of It, for Love?" and "Lines Written to an Unknown Audience, Waiting for the Night's First Act" both originally appeared in his chapbook, *The Influence of Pigeons on Architecture*, Yellow Pepper Press, 2004. TIM HEMPFIELD: "Godzilla!" first appeared in *Storyteller Magazine*. MIKE JAMES: "Lines Dictated at Kazansky's Deli" first appeared in *Bathtub Gin* and subsequently in *Alternate Endings*, Foothills Press, 2007. MARC JAMPOLE: "Schoenberg's Second Conversion" appeared in *Music from Words*, Bellday Books, 2007. MIKE KANE: "Prayer of Pulling Down Bricks" originally appeared in *Nimrod*. ROMELLA KITCHENS: "Morning Meditations" originally appeared in *Rune #1*, Robert Morris University, Spring 2007. MARGARET MENAMIN: "Kate Soffel Writes to Her Husband from Jail" first appeared in *Essential Tremors,* an online chapbook, 2005. CHRISTINE DOREIAN MICHAELS: "China Blue" first appeared in *No Choice but to Trust*, The Sanburg-Livesay Award. VIVIANA MIHELCIC: "Triumph" was previously published by the Famous Poets Society in 2005. STEPHEN MURABITO: "Blessings, Cursings: The Chained Shelves" is forthcoming in *The Lowering of the Body: The West Eighth Street Sequence*, Star Cloud Press, 2008. ED OCHESTER: "Pasta" first appeared in *Ploughshares* and *Unreconstructed: Poems Selected and New*, Autumn House Press, 2007. WALT PETERSON: "Shaking Hands with a Jackhammer" previously appeared in his chapbook *In the Waiting Room of the Speedy Muffler King*, Unfinished Monument Press, 1999. SANKAR ROY: "In Search of My New County" previously published in the chapbook *The House My Father Could Not Build*, Pudding House. JOANNE SAMRANEY: "Even at Five" was first published in *Main Street Rag*, 2007. RICHARD ST. JOHN: "Christmas Requiem" appeared in *The Pure Inconstancy of Grace*, Truman State University, 2005. MIKE SCHNEIDER: "Breath Through Bones" first appeard in *Passager*, Summer 2006. M.J. WASHINGTON: "What I Like About Home" first appeared in her chapbook, *The Words Just Jumped Right Out!*, Meeting of the Minds Publication, 2005. JUDY YOGMAN: "April" first appeard in *Squirrel Hill Magazine*. MICHAEL YOUNG: "Twilight Innings" first appeared in the *Pittsburgh Post-Gazette*. ANDRENA ZAWINSKI: "Driving the Laurels" first appeared in the *Bay Area Poets Coalition Anthology 23*, Berkeley and later online at the Bay Area Writing Project's *Digital Paper*.